Everything the Beginner Needs to Know to Invest Shrewdly

the text of this book is printed
on 100% recycled paper

Everything the Beginner Needs to Know to Invest Shrewdly

JEROME TUCCILLE

BARNES & NOBLE BOOKS

A DIVISION OF HARPER & ROW, PUBLISHERS

New York, Hagerstown, San Francisco, London

A hardcover edition of this book is published by Arlington House, Publishers.
It is here reprinted by arrangement.

First BARNES & NOBLE BOOKS edition published 1979

ISBN: 0-06-463476-0

79 80 81 82 83 10 9 8 7 6 5 4 3 2 1

To my father, Salvatore J. Tuccille, who insisted that money was important when I didn't want to believe him.

Contents

Introduction

Several years ago I was thoroughly ignorant regarding the world of finance. I literally did not know the difference between a stock and a bond, and like most people in my situation, I was ashamed to admit this to anyone. This was an especially awkward position for me since my father was undergoing surgery for a serious illness, and his doctors did not give him much chance of recovery. My sister and I would have inherited a sizable portfolio of various securities—common and preferred stocks, corporate and municipal bonds, warrants, stock and bond funds—and, so far as we were concerned, it would have been the same as handling a bundle of papers written in Sanskrit. Fortunately, my father eventually did recover after six operations, defying overwhelming odds stacked against him, and spared both my sister and myself the additional agony of acquiring an instantaneous crash education in securities investments.

Shortly afterward I found myself between jobs, and I was scouting around for a suitable opportunity requiring the skills of a freelance writer with a sales background. I opened the classified section of the Sunday *New York Times* and saw that a major brokerage firm was advertising for applicants in a stockbroker training program. The bells went off inside my head. Here was a golden opportunity for me: a chance to re-join the ranks of the gainfully employed and to acquire a sorely needed education at the same time.

Me? A stockbroker? The whole idea was bizarre. Someone who thought that such terms as *yield, P/E ratio, dividends, interest, primary issue, prime rate, margin requirements, puts, calls,* etc., were part of the Greek language, applying for a job as a stockbroker? Well, I thought, why not give it a shot?

To make a long story short, I did apply, I was hired, and I have been advising people on how to invest their money since 1975. I still have not gotten completely used to the idea, and have to pinch myself every now and then to make sure I am not dreaming. I have actually become a professional in a field I always believed I "had no head for." My world was books and articles. How could I ever understand the alien world of securities and investments? Yet, in an amazingly short period of time, I was able to learn all I had ever wanted to know about this world (but was too ashamed to ask) and then some.

Since becoming a stockbroker ("account executive," or "registered rep," as we are labeled in the trade), I have come in contact with hundreds of people in precisely the same position I was in only a few short years ago: widows who suddenly find themselves the heirs of a substantial estate, and panic because they don't understand the first thing about it; women in general who think they should know more about investments, but are too embarrassed to ask questions for fear of being laughed at ("Just like a woman." "What do women know about these things anyway?"); people suddenly coming into large sums of money who haven't the faintest notion of what to do with their new-found wealth; others tired of leaving cash in a bank account at low interest and falling behind because of inflation; and dozens of variations on the above.

All of them are looking for help, and most are too embarrassed to admit how little they know. My first reaction is to try to put them immediately at ease and assure them they are not stupid because they haven't taken the time to learn about a

14

field that seems enormously complicated from the outside looking in. Most professional money managers will say that a broker's clients are reflections of himself, and I guess it is no surprise that my own clientele is composed to a great extent of people similar to those described above.

Finally, I decided that someone ought to write a book tailored to the needs of those who know nothing about investments. Dozens of books are available for the sophisticated investor looking to take advantage of tax shelters, commodity straddles, and other loopholes in the tax laws, and there are scores of books on how to make money in various markets: gold, options, bonds, stocks, ad infinitum. But, amazingly enough, no one has yet written a brief, easy-to-read beginner's primer, starting with such basic questions as "What is a stock?" and "What is a bond?" and taking the reader along by the hand, step by step, to a point where he has received a simple fundamental education in the world of financial investments.

That's exactly what this book is—a basic education written in layman's language, starting from A and going all the way to Z. It is not a book for the sophisticated investor. I am assuming that you are someone like myself a few years back who knows absolutely nothing about stocks, bonds, money market instruments, options, and other investment vehicles. The few books already on the market that claim to do this are sluggish reading, and get bogged down in unnecessary (and often obsolete) details as you get into them. In writing this book I have avoided all nonessential information and concentrated on the fundamentals. When you finish you will know all the basics you have to know in order to invest your money shrewdly.

If this book works the way it should, it can be taken as an informal introductory course on securities investments. It can serve also as a constant companion, a ready reference you can consult as you need it. If, for instance, you are looking for information on calls, you can turn to part three, "Your Investment Dictionary," for a brief definition. Should you require more detail than is provided there, you can turn to the table of contents or the index to locate a more comprehensive treatment of the subject.

To start with, of course, you should read the book slowly from beginning to end as often as you like, letting the facts gradually sink in. Regard it as a casual, ongoing dialogue between friends. There is no need to "finish it" and rush on to something else.

Since this is a book on *securities* investments, I have not covered commodities, which is a subject worthy of book-length treatment by itself. Commodities will be dealt with in my next book, along with more sophisticated investment strategies, monetary and fiscal policies and their effect on inflation and interest rates, and broader economic concepts.

Part One:

Understanding Securities

1

What Is a Stock?

Common Stock

Any book on investments for the beginner should start, logically, with a discussion of stocks. What are stocks? What do they represent?

There are two basic ways a corporation raises money to finance its operations. It issues debt securities called bonds, and equity securities called stocks. Bonds will be covered in chapter two, so let's concentrate on equities here.

An *equity security* represents ownership in the corporation that issued it. The two broad classes of equities that corporations may issue are common stock and preferred stock. All corporations issue common stock and some issue preferred stock as well.

In a privately owned corporation, ordinarily the shares of common stock may be sold or disposed of only with the consent of the other shareholders. In the case of a publicly owned corporation, there is a *liquid market*, that is, its shares of common stock can be bought and sold on an open market without the consent of the other shareholders. Privately owned corporations do not offer their stock for sale to the public. Publicly owned corporations do, and these are the stocks that are traded regularly.

Common stock represents shares of ownership in a particular corporation. The shareholders are the actual owners of the corporation, proportionate to the number of shares they hold. In most cases, owners of common stock in a publicly owned corporation are entitled to certain basic rights:

(1) They have the right to sell or give away their shares without permission of the corporation. Their stock is freely transferable to anyone who wants to buy it or receive it as a gift.

(2) They usually have the preemptive right to maintain their proportionate share of the ownership in the corporation. For example, if the ABC Corporation has one million shares of common stock outstanding, and you own 10,000 shares of ABC common stock, you own one percent of all the outstanding shares of common stock. If ABC decides to issue 100,000 *new* shares of common stock, the company has to offer you the opportunity to buy 1000 of the new shares before they are offered to the public so that you can maintain your proportionate share of ownership. You can, of course, refuse to buy these new shares if you don't want them. This right guarantees to stockholders that their ownership in the company will not be diminished against their wishes.

(3) They have the right to a proportionate share of the corporation's earnings *after* the interest on bonds and dividends on preferred stocks have been paid. The corporation may pay a part of its earnings to owners of common stock in the form of dividends. The first obligation, however, is to its bond holders, the second, to preferred stock owners. A percentage of the company's remaining profits may be paid to common stockholders, and the balance reinvested for production and corporate growth.

(4) They have a right of limited access to the corporation's books. For the most part, common stockholders have the right to examine the minutes of meetings of the board of directors, and the right to examine the list of stockholders. Usually, this

right is not exercised unless the performance of the corporation's management declines seriously.

(5) They generally have the right to vote for corporate directors and on major policy decisions. Corporations usually provide for either statutory or cumulative voting. With statutory voting rights, if you own 500 shares of common stock in a particular company, you may cast up to 500 votes for each position. In cumulative voting, if there are three positions to be filled, you could cast 1500 votes (three positions × 500 shares) for any particular candidate if you choose, instead of dividing your votes equally among candidates for the three positions. Most U.S. corporations provide for the statutory system. Most investors cannot be present at stockholders meetings to vote in person, so owners of common stock receive proxy statements, which they can fill out and return by mail so their vote can be registered.

(6) They have the right to a proportionate share of the corporation's assets *after* bondholders' claims and preferred stockholders' claims have been paid if the company should be liquidated under bankruptcy proceedings. Again, a corporation's obligation is to bondholders first and preferred stockholders next. If there is anything left after these claims have been settled, owners of common stock will share it proportionately to the number of shares they own.

These, then, are the basic rights ordinarily guaranteed to all owners of common stock: They can buy or sell their stock freely or give it away. They have the right to maintain their proportionate share in the ownership of the corporation. They usually have a right to their proportionate share of the dividends if dividends are paid on the common stock. They have limited access to the corporation's books. They can vote. They are entitled to a share of the assets in bankruptcy proceedings if there is anything left. It is good to have a working knowledge of your rights when you buy shares of common stock.

In part two, "How to Invest," we will talk about how to go about selecting different kinds of common stock to suit your particular financial needs—picking stocks for dividends, growth, etc.

Another item the investor should be aware of when buying common stock is the *par value* assigned to the stock. When stock is issued there may or may not be a par value designation on the face of the certificate. You should know that this is essentially a meaningless figure as far as the investor in *common* stock is concerned. It is an arbitrary figure created by the corporation for bookkeeping purposes. It is important for the corporation's financial statements only. (It is a different story for the investor in preferred stock. See below.)

The only dollar value of concern to the common-stock investor is the *market value* of the stock. This is the price a stock can be bought or sold for, and it is usually substantially different than the par value. What a stock is worth at any given moment is strictly a function of the marketplace. What people are willing to pay for it and what they are willing to sell it for determines its current market value.

Occasionally a corporation will declare a stock *split*. If a corporation has one million shares of common stock outstanding selling for, say, $100 a share, it may declare that on such-and-such a date the stock will split two-for-one. This means that on the date indicated, the company will have 2 million shares outstanding at half the par value, and each stockholder will have twice as many shares as he had before the split. The expectation is that the market value of the shares will find a level relative to the increased number of shares outstanding. In this case, the two-for-one split will result in a market value of roughly $50 a share. By declaring a split, a corporation hopes that the lower price per share will make its common stock more attractive and more affordable to the investing public. The hope is that more people will buy it at the lower price and the stock will, consequently, continue to rise in value. This is important to both potential investors and current shareholders, who will both be affected by the future price movement of the stock. It should be pointed out, however, that there is no guarantee that the stock will go up. If there were, we could all get rich by buying stock before a split and watching it take off afterward. Only a novice investor would jump in to take advantage of a split without investigating other aspects of the corporation. The same principles hold true for three-for-one splits, three-for-two, or any other ratio. Just adjust the numbers accordingly.

Another reason for a stock split may be to allow a corporation to qualify for listing on a stock exchange. One requirement for listing, for example, may be a minimum of one million publicly held shares outstanding. Assuming that a corporation meets all other requirements but has only half a million shares out, it could declare a two-for-one split to get itself listed.

A corporation may declare a *reverse split*, which is just the opposite of what was described above. A company with a million shares of common stock outstanding may find itself in financial difficulty, and the market value of its stock may drop to, say, $3 per share. By declaring a four-for-one reverse split, the corporation will then have 250,000 shares outstanding with an expected market value of somewhere around $12 each. The company hopes to make the stock look less risky and, therefore, more attractive to the investing public, thereby bringing in more money and improving its financial position. A listed company, however, runs the risk of being de-listed by an exchange if its number of shares falls below the minimum requirement after the reverse split. We will talk more about listed and over-the-counter stocks a bit later.

Instead of declaring a split or a reverse split, a corporation may declare a *stock dividend*. A 10 percent stock dividend means that for every ten shares of common stock outstanding, one new share will be given as a dividend to the shareholders. A split does *not* create new assets; a stock dividend does. If a corporation with 100,000 shares of common stock out declares a 10 percent stock dividend, it then has 110,000 shares out at the *same* par value. It is a different bookkeeping procedure, which creates an actual increase in the company's assets. If you owned 100 shares of stock in this company before the stock divided was declared, you would now own 110 shares without charge to you.

Corporations sometimes pay another form of dividend to their shareholders called a *property dividend*. If you own stock in a parent corporation that wants to divest itself of stock it holds in a subsidiary, it may pay out this subsidiary stock as a dividend. Or the parent may want to establish the subsidiary as an independent spin-off company. It can do this by issuing stock in the spin-off as a dividend to the shareholders.

This covers the pertinent information you should know before buying common stock, what it is, what rights it provides, the kinds of occurrences that could affect your interests as a stockholder.

Preferred Stock

Like common stock, *preferred stock* is also an equity security; that is, it represents shares of ownership in the corporation that issues it. While all publicly owned corporations issue common stock, only some issue preferred stock.

Perhaps the best way to explain the characteristics of preferred stock is to outline the differences between preferred and common stock. The dividends on common stock may fluctuate from year to year, while preferred-stock dividends are paid at a fixed rate if the company's earnings are sufficient to cover them. For example, if an investor buys a preferred stock for $50 and the stated dividend is $4 per year, the company is obligated to pay the preferred stock dividend in full before any dividends are paid out on common stock. Common stock dividends will be paid if they are covered by earnings, but only after the preferred stockholders have been taken care of.

Another major difference is that par value is important to investors in preferred stock because it is the figure upon which the dividend is calculated. The dividend may be stated as 7 percent of, say, $100 par value, which means you, the investor, will receive $7 per year for every share of this particular preferred stock you own. The fixed rate of return can also be stated in terms of dollars, so many dollars per year for each share.

One more difference between preferred stock and common stock is that preferred stockholders usually do not have voting rights. This situation can be changed, however, if a corporation defaults on its dividend payments because of declining earnings. According to some corporate charters, preferred stock becomes voting stock if the dividends are missed for a set number of quarters. This provision is required by several exchanges in order for a corporation to become listed.

Before you decide to invest in preferred stock, you should be aware that this type of security is sold with certain features. Not all preferred stocks carry these features. Some have all, others none, others yet may have any combination of them.

The first feature we will talk about is the *prior dividend* provision. This gives one class of preferred stock priority over subsequent issues of preferred sold by the corporation. For example, if the DEF Corporation issues a Class A preferred with a 7 percent rate of return and then a later, Class B, preferred with a 7.5 percent rate, DEF must cover the payment on its A preferred before it pays anything out on the B. The DEF Class A preferred is called its *prior preferred*.

Second, some preferreds have a *participating dividend* provision. This means that preferred stockholders are entitled to additional dividends if the amount set aside for common stock dividends exceeds a certain amount. It usually works like this. Once a corporation has paid the interest due to its bondholders, the fixed dividends due to its preferred shareholders, and the dividends due its common stockholders, it may find itself with additional earnings that it would rather pay out in dividends than reinvest in production. When this happens, these additional earnings are divided among both preferred and common stockholders. Preferreds sold with this feature are called *participating preferreds*.

A third feature of some preferred stock is a *cumulative divi-*

dend provision. If a corporation's earnings decline drastically, it may not be able to pay the dividends to its preferred stockholders. The stockholder could lose these dividends completely until the company is operating profitably again. As an additional protection for the investor, some corporations issue *cumulative preferred* stock. This guarantees that the preferred dividends in arrears must be paid before any common stock dividends are paid. If a company misses its payments on cumulative preferred for a quarter, it has to pay that quarter's dividends plus the latest quarter's dividends before resuming payment of its common stock dividends.

One of the most attractive features a preferred stock can have is a provision for conversion. *Convertible preferred* stock can be traded for a set number of common stock shares in the issuing company at the investor's discretion. As a general rule, common stock fluctuates in value more widely than preferred stock. Common stock is considered to have more growth potential, while preferred stock is bought primarily for income, for its high dividend payments. If the common stock of a particular corporation moves up sharply, however, convertible preferred stock which can be exchanged for it usually moves up sharply as well. It tends to track the price movement of the common. For this reason preferred stock is not often exchanged for common. The conversion ratio ordinarily is balanced by speculation in the preferred stock. So we can see that this conversion feature provides the investor with growth potential in the preferred stock as well as high current income.

To sum up the things you should know about preferred stock before investing in it, preferred stock is an equity security (ownership in the corporation); it carries a fixed rate of return which takes priority over common-stock dividends; its par value is important since the dividend is often stated as a percentage of par; and it does not give you voting rights except under dire circumstances. Various types of preferred stock include: prior preferred, participating preferred, cumulative preferred, and convertible preferred.

Now we are ready to talk about the way stock is purchased.

Buying and Selling Stocks

Stocks are bought and sold in round lots and odd lots. A *round lot* is shares of stock in multiples of 100; 100, 300, 600, 800, 1000, and 1500 shares of stock are all round lots. An *odd lot* is less than 100 shares; 50, 60, and 75 shares of stock are odd lots. One hundred and fifty shares of stock is a round lot of 100 and an odd lot of 50. Three hundred and thirty shares is a round lot of 300 and an odd lot of 30. There are rare circumstances where a particular stock may trade in round lots of 10 or 50, but for most purposes, the above is all you need to know about round lots and odd lots.

In parts two and three we will talk about commission schedules and whether it is better to buy stock in round lots or odd lots. But, for the moment, let us just familiarize ourselves with the terms.

The great majority of stock transactions are *market orders* to buy or sell. When you buy stock "at the market" it means you are buying it at the best currently available price. A particular stock may be trading at 56¼ a share at the moment. If you want to buy it at the market you will pay about that price, but you won't be sure exactly what until the order is executed. When you buy at the market, you are willing to buy at the current market price, whatever it happens to be.

The same principle holds true when you are selling. You are willing to sell your stock at the market for the best price you can currently get. There are no guarantees of price in a market order.

Another common type of order is a *limit order*. If you wanted to buy that same stock we mentioned a moment earlier which was trading at 56¼, but you wanted to make sure you did not pay more than, say, 56½ for it, you would put a limit on it at 56½. In this case you would be certain that you would not pay more than you want to for the stock. You would pay 56½ or less for it if the market warranted it. You could make this a *day order*, which means the order will be automatically canceled at the end of the day's trading if the order cannot be executed. (The stock might jump to 56¾ right after you place the order, in which case you could not get the stock for your limit or less.) Or you could make it a *good-till-canceled*, or *open, order*, which means your order will stay in effect for thirty days. If at any time within the thirty days the stock falls within your limit, your order could be executed. If it cannot, your order will automatically be canceled when the thirty days are up. The danger with a limit order is that you could miss the market; that is, if the stock is moving up sharply and your limit is too low, you will not get the stock and you will lose out on any profit. If you are certain you want the stock, you should place either a market order or a limit slightly higher than the current value of the stock.

The same holds true when you are selling at a limit. You want to sell some stock, but you want to be sure you don't get less than a certain price for it. So you put in a limit, which means you will get your price *or better* if the stock should be sold. Again, if you really want to sell your stock *now,* you should put in a market order or a limit slightly below the current price of the stock.

There are several other kinds of orders that can get a bit complicated and are used infrequently, so we won't bother covering them here. Later on, when we talk about investment strategies, I will mention some of them. But there is one other type of order called a *stop order* that you should have some working knowledge of before buying a stock. The idea behind a stop order is very simple. Suppose you have bought a stock for $30 a share and it has risen to $42 a share. You have a nice profit, but you don't want to sell yet since you think your stock might go higher. On the other hand, you don't want to see your stock fall back to $30 again and lose the paper profit you have at present (it is not a dollar profit until you actually sell). What you might do in this case is call your broker and tell him to sell the stock if it falls to $40. This way you are guaranteeing yourself approximately a $10 profit since the stock will be sold at the market if the stock should start to fall. Your broker will place a *stop order* to sell at this price ($40) only if the stock should fall to this level. The danger here is that the stock could fall to $40 and your shares will be sold, and then the stock could turn around and continue higher again. You are running the risk of missing out on a potential higher move when you enter a stop order.

These, then, are the main things you should be concerned about when buying or selling stock. You will be buying or selling in round lots or odd lots. You will be buying or selling at the market or at a limit. In addition, you might put in a stop order to safeguard some paper profits.

These principles pertain to both common and preferred stock.

Listed and Over-the-Counter Stocks

All stocks are either listed or unlisted. A *listed stock* is one that has qualified for listing on one of the securities exchanges; the New York Stock Exchange (NYSE) and the American Stock Exchange (AMEX) are the two national exchanges, and there are a number of regional exchanges, including the Boston, Midwest, and Pacific exchanges. Listing on a securities exchange means that a corporation is traded there after having satisfied certain requirements established by the exchange.

To qualify for listing, a corporation must furnish pertinent information regarding its earnings, financial condition, number of shares it has outstanding, types of stock it has issued, and other details which we need not go into here. When a stock is traded on an exchange, it has satisfied the minimum requirements set forth by that particular exchange. Some stocks have multiple listing, which means they are traded on several exchanges, and this trend has been accelerating in recent years.

Listing on an exchange provides certain advantages for the investor. The exchanges serve as a reasonably continuous market for a stock. They do not guarantee that a stock will be bought or sold once you place an order, but the continuous market makes it almost certain that most orders will be executed. For this reason, listed stocks are said to have good marketability. The exchanges also protect the investor from fraud since they establish rules for trading and are empowered to take disciplinary action in case of any violations.

All stocks which are not traded on an exchange are bought and sold *over the counter*. The OTC market, as it is called, does not have a physical location. These transactions are made over the telephone by means of an "electronic market." Various brokers and securities dealers make a market in different OTC stocks; that is, they deal in large blocks of shares of different unlisted stocks they are willing to buy from and sell to other brokers for a negotiated price. These broker-dealers making a market in OTC stocks communicate with one another via a nationwide computerized telecommunications network. At any given moment a broker in one firm can check his quote machine to find out which firms are making a market in any given OTC stock. He can then call the firm offering the best current price for the stock and negotiate a transaction for his firm's client.

The great majority of stocks traded in the United States are bought and sold in the OTC market. When a stock is traded OTC it does not necessarily mean that it cannot qualify for listing on one of the exchanges. Many top-quality corporations in every conceivable industry decide against listing their stocks for a number of reasons. Some do not feel that they need a physical marketplace since there is already a continuous market for their stocks. Others may not want to comply with the procedures and put up with the paperwork involved in getting themselves listed. Traditionally many bank stocks, insurance stocks, and foreign stocks have traded over the counter. On the other hand, corporations which cannot meet the minimum requirements for listing on an exchange are also traded OTC. The OTC stock listings in the financial pages of newspapers are not complete; only the more actively traded securities are listed there each day since it is not physically possible to mention all of them. Your broker will have a more complete list.

Having learned all this, you should note that there is currently a plan in the works to create a central marketplace. The details have not been completed yet, but in all probability the new central marketplace will be patterned to one extent or another on the OTC market. More and more stocks are now being traded off the tape, off the floors of the exchanges, in what amounts to a new OTC market. Eventually the entire marketplace for stocks will be computerized, as it is becoming more of a negotiated market. This does not mean that the exchanges themselves will be eliminated; their function will still be to list corporations that meet their minimum requirements. But it does mean that the method by which you buy and sell stocks will change. Sooner or later your broker will be able to guarantee you an execution off the machine just as he does today in the OTC market. He will pull the price off the quote machine and confirm the trade with you while you are still on the phone with him. Some firms are doing this already.

To sum up this section, when you are buying or selling stocks you should know if your stocks are listed or OTC. If they are listed you should know where they are listed: NYSE, AMEX, etc. You should also know what grade of stocks you are dealing in: investment grade, growth, speculative. We will talk more about this when we discuss investment strategies.

You now have a basic working knowledge of both common and preferred stocks.

2

What Is a Corporate Bond?

As we discussed in the last chapter, a corporation raises money in addition to its earnings primarily by issuing both equity and debt securities. We have already covered equities, so in this chapter we will talk about debt obligations.

Debt securities represent money loaned to a corporation by investors in corporate bonds. *Bonds* are certificates of the corporation's indebtedness. These certificates state the corporation's obligation to pay back a specific amount of money on a specific date. They also state a corporation's obligation to pay the investor a specific interest for the use of his funds. When you buy a bond you are lending a corporation money for a set period of time at a fixed annual interest rate.

When a corporation issues a debt security it can be either secured or unsecured. *Secured debt securities* are backed by various kinds of assets of the corporation, while *unsecured debt securities* are backed only by the reputation, credit record, and financial stability of the corporation.

Bonds are referred to as long-term debt securities; they mature in periods of more than twenty years. That is, when the corporation borrows your money, it agrees to pay you back more than twenty years later. Other kinds of debt securities, which are sold primarily to institutions, are short-term obligations called notes. One kind of note—commerical paper—matures in 270 days or less. Longer-term notes mature in periods of one to twenty years. You should be aware of the differences between bonds and notes, but in this chapter, we will concentrate on bonds.

Secured and Unsecured Bonds

Bonds, as we mentioned a moment ago, can be either secured or unsecured (notes are always unsecured). In the case of a secured bond, the terms of the legal agreement between the corporation and the investor are usually printed on the bond certificate itself. This agreement is also referred to as a *deed of trust*, or an *indenture*.

One type of secured bond is a *mortgage bond*, which is backed by real estate and physical assets of the corporation. The various assets used to secure the bonds ordinarily have a market value greater than the principal amount of the bonds, that is, the money owed by the company on these particular bonds. If the corporation develops financial problems and defaults on the bonds, the assets used to back them must then be sold to pay off the mortgage bondholders. The indenture will also indicate whether the mortgage bonds are open-end or closed-end. If they are *closed-end*, the assets can only be used to secure these particular bonds; if *open-end*, owners of subsequent mortgage bonds issued by the company will have equal claim on the assets in case of default.

A second type of secured bond is the *equipment trust certificate*, which is issued mostly by railroads and occasionally by airlines and other transportation companies. These bonds mature serially, that is, part of the debt is paid off each year for a set period of time, with a different interest rate for each year of maturity. If you decided to buy one with a maturity of only ten years, you would get a certain annual interest for that period. If you went out twenty years (bought one with a twenty-year maturity) you would, of course, get a higher rate of interest since your money was being held longer. (From this we can see that there are exceptions to the rule that bonds mature in twenty years or more. Sometimes the distinction between a bond and a long-term note seems arbitrary. As a basic rule, however, remember that a *note* is a short-term *unsecured* debt security.)

The assets backing an equipment trust security are the rolling stock of the corporation. A railroad actually places its engines and other rolling stock in trust to secure the bonds. These bonds can be issued under either the Philadelphia plan, the most common approach, or the New York plan. Under the Philadelphia plan, a trustee retains title to the rolling stock and equipment of the railroad until all dividends and principal have been paid in full. Only when its entire obligation has been satisfied does title pass back to the corporation. If the corporation should default on any of its payments beforehand, the trustee may rent or sell the equipment to pay off the bondholders. With the New York plan, a proportionate part of the equipment is returned to the corporation as it retires the debt. This means that, as the corporation pays back the bondholders each year as the bonds mature, title to the equipment gradually passes to the company. In effect, under the New York plan the corporation is paying off a mortgage and building up equity in the equipment.

A third type of secured bond is the *collateral trust bond*. In this case, a corporation owns securities in other companies, which can be either subsidiaries or independent companies. The parent company then issues bonds that are backed by the securities it owns in these other firms. The market value of these securities usually exceeds the *face amount* (the principal) of the bonds by at least 25 percent. As in the case of other secured bonds, an independent trustee is appointed to protect the interests of the investor.

An unsecured bond is one which is backed by the reputation and financial record of the company. These bonds are known as *debentures* and they are issued primarily by major corporations which do not invest heavily in property or fixed assets. Debentures represent an unconditional promise by the corporation to pay the stated interest annually and the principal (face amount of the bond) on the date of maturity. Since these bonds are a promise not guaranteed by physical assets, they are issued by corporations in sound financial condition. A *subordinated debenture* is one that gives precedence to all other bonds issued by the corporation. If a company has previous bonds outstanding and it needs to raise additional money, it could issue a subordinated debenture. Interest must be paid to the other bondholders before it is paid to the holders of subordinated debentures. (Claims of investors in subordinated debentures, of course, take priority over those of both preferred and common stockholders.)

Corporate bonds, then, are long-term debt securities issued by corporations. Interest on them has precedence over dividends paid to stockholders. Bonds carry face amounts (usually $1000), and they pay an annual rate of interest (usually semiannually). They can be either secured (mortgage bonds, equipment trust certificates, collateral trust bonds) or unsecured (debentures and subordinated debentures).

Callable Bonds

Corporate bonds can be either *callable* or *noncallable*. *Callability* is a feature which permits a corporation to *redeem* its bonds (pay off the principal) before maturity if it so desires. For example, suppose you buy ABC 8s of '06—ABC bonds paying 8 percent annually until 2006 when the company is obligated to pay back the principal amount of the bonds. Before 2006, however, interest rates may fall to 7 percent for similar-quality bonds. ABC knows it can issue new bonds at the lower interest rate instead of continuing to pay you 8 percent a year. If the 8s of '06 are callable, ABC may decide to call them in and re-fund its debt. This means that the company will re-tire the bonds early and pay back the principal, then reissue new bonds at a lower interest rate. However, the corporation has to pay you a *call price* to do this. If the face value of the bonds is $1000 (expressed as 100), ABC may have to pay back 102½, or $1025, for the right to redeem them early (although this is not always so). When you buy callable bonds, the call price will be indicated as well as the years of callability. Bonds maturing in 2006 may be callable starting in 1996 but not be-fore then if that is the first call date.

Some corporations establish a *sinking fund* expressly for this purpose. This means that a company allocates a percentage of its earnings to a special trust fund in order to keep retiring a portion of its debt. This is also regarded as an added protec-tion for the investor, who is assured that a cash reserve is be-ing systematically established to cover the company's financial obligations. (It should be noted that a few preferred stocks are also callable for the same reason that bonds are callable.)

Convertible Bonds

Convertible bonds can be exchanged for the company's common stock at the discretion of the investor. In a few instances the bonds may be convertible to preferred rather than common stock. The ratio of conversion varies from one bond to an-other, according to the terms set forth at the time the bonds are issued. To use a simple illustration, a bond with a $1000 face value may be convertible into 50 shares of the company's common stock. The conversion ratio is 50 to 1. If the stock is selling at 20, it is at *parity* with the bonds ($20 \times 50 = $1000). But if the stock moves up to 25, the price of the convertible bond will tend to track the price movement of the stock. Parity now will be $1250 (quoted as 125, remember), since $25 \times $50 = $1250. (It is important to understand that par and parity are not the same; *parity* means that the convertible bond and the stock are priced in relation to their conversion ratio.) In this case, the bond will be selling at a $250 premium. If the stock dropped to 18 and the bond to 90 ($18 × 50 = $900), the bond would be selling at a discount.

Only about 5 percent of all issued bonds are convertible. Most investors in bonds are looking for income, so they look for the highest interest rates currently available with minimum risk to their principal; but convertible bonds usually offer lower interest rates with greater growth potential than non-convertible bonds. They offer a combination of income and growth, as do preferreds, and some investors find them attractive for this reason. (*Income* is money you receive as interest and/or dividends, while *growth* is the appreciation in value of the securities themselves.) Some investors also buy bonds selling at a discount for a combination of growth and income, as we will see in part two.

Convertible bonds, like convertible preferreds, are rarely converted into the underlying stock for which they can be exchanged. In reality, conversion ratios are far more complex than in the example given above, and since convertibles tend to track the price of the underlying common there is usually no benefit for the average investor in actually converting. (There is something called arbitrage whereby wealthy, seasoned investors can take advantage of momentary spreads in the market, but this is too involved for our purposes here.)

Bringing ourselves further up to date, we have discovered so far that corporate bonds are long-term debt securities, secured or unsecured, callable or noncallable, convertible or nonconvertible.

Bankruptcy Proceedings and More

We have already discussed the main characteristics of corporate bonds. Before proceeding to the actual buying and selling of them, however, there are a few more items you should be aware of.

First, *bankruptcy* procedures. When a corporation falls into dire financial straits and is no longer capable of meeting its obligations to investors, it may go into one of two chapters under the federal bankruptcy laws, Chapter X or Chapter XI. Of the two, Chapter X is the more serious.

Chapter X involves total readjustment of the corporation's secured bonds. A court appoints a trustee, or receiver, to make a complete review of the company's assets and work out a plan of liquidation. The company is managed by the receiver until the liquidation is accomplished. Chapter XI is a simple corporate reorganization involving adjustments of unsecured bonds. A corporation going through financial difficulty submits a plan to the court for adjusting its obligation to debenture holders. The court consults with corporate management and representatives for the investors, and makes a determination. In some cases, the maturity date might be extended another five or ten years to give the company more time to resolve its problems.

A corporation undergoing bankruptcy proceedings might issue *income*, or *adjustment*, bonds to raise immediate capital. These bonds take priority over all other obligations of the company, and the interest on them is guaranteed only if the corporation begins to earn profits again. Obviously, these are high-risk bonds, issued only in the most extreme circumstances, and are not bought by the average investor.

Another kind of bond you might hear about occasionally is a *guaranteed bond*. This is a bond guaranteed by a company other than the one that issues it. Sometimes a parent corporation with a higher credit rating than a subsidiary will guarantee the subsidiary's bonds, enabling the smaller company to issue bonds at a lower interest rate.

The last item which we will cover here is bonds issued in series. Earlier we mentioned serial maturity dates, bonds sold at the same time maturing in different years. *Series* bonds are just the opposite. They are bonds issued at *different* times maturing in the *same* year. A corporation may plan a long period of expansion over, say, the next thirty years. To raise capital along the way, it may issue new bonds every five years, all maturing on the same date thirty years from the first issue.

You now have a working knowledge of what bonds are and what the different kinds of bonds represent. Next we will talk about buying and selling them.

Buying and Selling Corporate Bonds

Like stocks, corporate bonds are sold in round lots and odd lots. However, the distinction here is a bit more arbitrary than is the case with stocks. Traditionally, blocks of 100 bonds (face value, $100,000) have been considered round lots and smaller amounts, odd lots. But lately, a few brokerage houses have been treating blocks of 250 bonds as round lots. This is mostly academic, though, since few investors can afford to spend $100,000, let alone $250,000, on securities. Round lots are of more concern to banks, insurance companies, other institutions, and extremely wealthy individual investors. For the average investor, it is enough to know that bonds usually come out with a $1000 face value (although there are some smaller units known as *baby bonds,* which have face values of less than $1000) and that you buy them in amounts you can afford.

Like stocks, bonds are also listed or unlisted. The more actively traded bonds on the New York and American stock exchanges are listed in the financial pages of newspapers. As in the case of stocks, however, most bonds are unlisted and are traded over the counter.

Most corporate bonds today are sold in fully *registered* form. When you buy these bonds, they are registered in your name (or names), and when the bonds mature the interest and principal are paid directly to you. *Unregistered* bonds are not registered in anyone's name. This is the usual form with municipal bonds, which we will discuss in chapter six. Unregistered bonds come equipped with coupons attached to them which you clip at set intervals and submit in order to receive your interest payments. These bonds are considered negotiable since the name of the owner is not printed on the bond certificate. Since the income from corporate bonds is taxable and there is no benefit to having them unregistered, most people buy them in registered form.

Although most bonds are issued with a face, or par, value of $1000, bond prices do fluctuate in the market. The interest a bond pays at par is called its *coupon rate*, or *nominal yield*. The ABC 8s of '06 mentioned earlier pay $80 a year for every $1000 of face value. But if you should buy the bonds at a premium (more than $1000) or a discount (less than $1000), your current yield will not be 8 percent. For example, if these bonds should fall to a current market value of 80 ($800), their current yield will be 10 percent—$80 per year for an $800 investment equals a 10 percent yield. Similarly, someone paying $1200 for the bonds will receive a current yield of 6.67 percent.

The third yield measurement for bonds, after nominal yield and current yield, is *yield to maturity*, or YTM. This measurement takes into consideration the capital gain or loss the investor will have when the bonds are redeemed at maturity. The person who buys the bonds mentioned above at $800, in addition to receiving a current yield of 10 percent, will get back $1000 if he holds the bonds to maturity. Consequently, this investor will have a capital gain of $200 on top of his annual interest. The individual paying $1200 for the bonds will have a $200 capital loss at maturity when he gets back face value for them. There is a fairly intricate formula used to calculate YTM. Your broker, however, will have a bond-basis book which takes care of the mathematics. By referring to the appropriate table he will be able to come up with this figure for you.

To summarize what we have discussed so far about buying and selling corporate bonds, in most cases they are issued with a face value of $1000. Bond prices fluctuate with the market, so at any given time they may be trading at par, at a premium, or at a discount. In all probability, you will be buying them in registered form. And you will want to know what the nominal, or coupon, yield is, as well as the current yield and the yield to maturity.

Interest Rates and Bond Prices

There are many reasons why interest rates rise and fall, most of them related to monetary and fiscal policies established by the government. Your main concern as an investor is the effect that interest rates have on the price fluctuations of bonds.

As a general rule of thumb, keep in mind that interest rates and bond prices move counter to each other. That is, when interest rates are going down bond prices will be going up, and when interest rates are going up bond prices will be going down. When most people hear this for the first time, they sometimes have difficulty understanding it. I know this was a problem for me. After all, I reasoned, when rates are going up bonds should become more valuable. More people will buy them and the prices should move up. But this is not how it works, and if you will follow me for a minute, I will try to explain what is actually happening.

Using our old friends again, the ABC 8s of '06, let us suppose that now, three years after they were issued, interest rates fall to an average of 7 percent for similar quality bonds. This means that, if the ABC Corporation were issuing those bonds today, it would only have to pay 7 percent interest on them instead of the 8 percent it offered a few years back. Newly issued bonds will be coming out with nominal yields of about 7 percent. Consequently, investors such as yourself will start buying the ABC 8s to get the higher interest rate. As the demand for the 8s increases, the price of the bonds will start moving up (excess demand plus limited supply equals higher prices). The bond prices will move up until the *current yield* on the

41

ABC 8s is about 7 percent. When these bonds reach a price of approximately $1140 (quoted as 114), they will no longer be especially attractive since the current yield will be 7 percent ($80 ÷ 1140 = 0.07), the same as the new bonds. Actually, when you calculate YTM, which takes your capital loss into consideration, the bonds will cease to be attractive at a lower price. But just keep the basic principle in mind. The prices of bonds fluctuate so that current yield and YTM are similar to newly issued bonds of equal quality.

Applying this principle, we can see that bond prices will fall when interest rates are moving higher. If interest rates rise to about 10 percent after the ABC 8s are issued, you will be more interested in buying the new 10 percent bonds instead of the old 8s. Demand for the old bonds will decline until they reach a level where they are competitive with the new issues.

If you understand this concept clearly now, you are far ahead of where I was at your stage. It is a simple, entirely reasonable principle, yet a bit elusive for some reason. Just keep going over these two examples until they begin to make good sense to you. Work out another example or two of your own if you find it helps. Once you have grasped it, you will understand the fundamental mechanics of the bond market and why it is so sensitive to interest rates—and, a bit more indirectly, to inflation.

Updating again, in addition to what we had already discussed about buying and selling bonds, we now know that they will be moving up in price when interest rates are falling, and down in price when interest rates are rising.

Rating Bonds

I have mentioned "bonds of similar quality" a few times. What exactly do I mean by this?

Like all investments, corporate bonds carry with them a certain degree of risk. A corporation may promise to pay you back your money. It may secure your investment with various kinds of assets. But you have no ironclad guarantee that you will get back your principal on the day the bonds are due. So, to varying degrees, it can be said that your money is at risk when you lend it to a corporation. For that is exactly what you are doing when you buy a bond, lending your money to a company. And when you do so there are risks that (1) the corporation will *default* on its interest or principal payments, (2) you may have difficulty selling them if there is no demand for the bonds you own, (3) interest rates will rise and you will be stuck with a relatively low yield—or, conversely, interest rates will *fall* and your bonds will be called so that the company can issue new bonds at the lower rate, and (4) inflation will soar to a level where the interest you are getting no longer represents a real return on your investment (for example, if inflation rises to 10 percent a year and you are getting only 8 percent annually, the value of your money is actually deteriorating by 2 percent a year without even taking taxes into consideration).

Investors have virtually no control over interest rates and inflation since they are, for the most part, reflections of the monetary and fiscal policies established in Washington, D.C. We can, however, take precautions against the first risk I mentioned: the risk of default. There are three major rating services that have developed systems for evaluating the quality of corporate bonds based on an analysis of a corporation's financial condition. The goal of this analysis is to determine the corporation's ability to meet interest payments in full and to pay back the principal when its bonds mature. These three services are *Standard and Poor's*, *Moody's*, and *Fitch's*. Standard and Poor and Fitch both issue the same letter rating for bonds: AAA, AA, A, BBB, BB, B, CCC, CC, C, DDD, DD, D. Moody's ratings correspond but are slightly different: Aaa, Aa, A, Baa, Ba, B, Caa, Ca, C (Moody does not issue D ratings).

AAA-, AA-, and A-rated bonds (Moody's Aaa, Aa, and A) are all high-quality bonds. Triple As are the best, while double and single As are slightly lower quality, but high-grade nonetheless.

BBB (Baa) bonds are considered to be good quality, and the next two levels are fair to speculative.

All Cs are poor quality bonds, and D ratings are given to bonds of companies in serious financial shape.

Someone looking for reasonable safety of principal and a relatively high yield will most likely not want to buy anything lower than a BBB or Baa bond. The bonds may have different ratings from different services, but usually they will not be more than a single grade apart; a bond may carry an A from Moody's and a BBB from S&P, for example. Lower grade bonds are for investors of a more *speculative* nature, who are willing to take a higher risk to get a higher yield. High quality bonds will have a lower yield since there is less risk involved. People are willing to buy them at lower yields because they are considered safer. There is a trade-off in effect here. You can trade safety for a higher interest rate, or you can trade interest for safety. It all depends on each individual investor, what his financial goals are, whether he feels more comfortable with a higher or lower risk investment. We will talk more about this when we move further along in the book.

Miscellaneous

Bond yields are sometimes quoted in *basis points*. A basis point is simply one-hundredth of one percent. So, a bond yielding 8.62 percent one day and 8.65 percent a week later has moved three basis points.

This is all you really need to know about the great mystery surrounding basis points. Each business develops its own language which sounds confusing until you take the time to learn it. The financial world is no exception: once you master a basic concept everything becomes a lot clearer.

As far as interest payments are concerned, most bonds pay

interest semiannually on either the first or fifteenth of the month. Bonds paying interest on March first and September first are called "M&S" bonds. M&S 15 bonds pay March fifteenth and September fifteenth. Bonds can be J&D (June first and December first) or J&D 15. J&J bonds pay January first and July first. A&O 15 bonds pay April fifteenth and October fifteenth. And so on for any other combination of months and dates. Just remember that the payments are six months apart.

When you buy bonds after an interest date, you will have to pay the previous owner *accrued interest*. For example, if on February first you buy a J&J bond (interest paid January first and July first) you owe the previous owner one month's accrued interest since he held the bond for one month into the current interest period. The accrued interest will be included on your bill when you pay for the bond. On July first you collect six months' interest. You paid one month's accrued interest, and the net result is five months' interest earned for the five months you owned the bond during the interest period.

If you happen to buy a bond on the day the interest falls due, you buy the bond *flat*; there is no accrued interest involved. Of course, if you are selling bonds, you are the one who collects the accrued interest if any is owed to you.

This concludes our session on corporate bonds. They are issued usually in denominations of $1000. They are long-term debt securities, secured or unsecured, callable or noncallable, convertible or nonconvertible. Most bonds are traded over the counter, and they trade at par, at a premium, or at a discount. Most likely you will buy them in registered form. You will want to know their coupon rate, their current yield, and yield to maturity. If interest rates go down your bonds will go up in price, and vice versa. You will also want to know how the bonds are rated before you buy them. And, finally, you will want to know on what dates you can expect to receive your interest check.

You now have a good working knowledge of two basic kinds of securities, stocks and bonds. Don't feel that you have to memorize everything we have discussed so far. Even seasoned brokers have to refer constantly to reference material before they can answer certain questions. The main thing is that you have a general understanding of what these securities are, what they represent, and how they are traded. You know a lot more now than you realize, certainly a lot more than most people, including many "experienced investors."

3

What Are Money Market Instruments?

When I first heard the term *money market instruments* I was completely baffled. What is a money market? What are these instruments I hear sophisticated investors talking about? How could I ever begin to understand this complicated world of financial investments? Starting from ground zero, it would take me a lifetime to learn. Or so I thought.

The reality of the situation is quite different. It is true that there is a lot of detail involved in understanding the investment world, but it seems far more complicated from the outside looking in than is actually the case. There is a fundamental logic at work here, and once you grasp the basic concepts everything begins to fall neatly in place.

Financial markets are divided into two sectors: the money market and the capital market. The difference between the two is the length of time your money is tied up. In the money market your capital is used for one year or less, and in the capital market your money is tied up for periods of longer than a year.

Let's talk about the *money market* first. It is a system established for governments, municipalities, corporations, other institutions, and individuals to finance their short-term cash needs by buying and selling debt securities that mature in one year or less. That's it in a nutshell. From your point of view as an investor, it means you are buying debt securities (lending your money) that will mature in one year or less. This period can be one year, it can be six months, 270 days, 90 days, 30 days, etc. Strictly speaking, there are four basic money market investments, or *money market instruments*. These are: treasury bills, bankers' acceptances, certificates of deposit, and commercial paper. Let's take them one at a time.

Treasury Bills

Treasury bills (T-bills) are debt securities issued by the United States government with maturities of three, six, and twelve months. They are considered to be completely safe investments since they are backed by the "full faith and credit" of the federal government. Treasury bills are usually sold in minimum denominations of $10,000.

Unlike corporate bonds, which pay periodic interest, treasury bills are sold on a *discount* basis. What this means in simple terms is that, since the holding period is so short, you pay less than face value for them. Upon maturity, the Treasury redeems them for face value. In other words, the interest on them is discounted in the price of the bills when you buy them. If you bought a ninety-day treasury bill worth $10,000, you would pay less than face value when you bought it and receive the full $10,000 upon maturity. Because these day-to-day calculations are so complicated, treasury bills are not quoted in dollar amounts. Instead, price quotes are given in terms of rate of return, what they will yield the investor for the time he will hold them.

Since treasury bills are backed by the full faith and credit of the federal government, and are therefore considered to be the safest of all money market instruments, their yields are normally lower than other money market securities. Interest rates on treasury bills generally move with other interest rates, although this movement is not perfectly synchronized. Rates are affected by supply, that is, the amount of borrowing done by the Treasury. Sharp increases or decreases in this borrowing will strongly influence the level of the interest rates. Also, expected changes in the Treasury's borrowing patterns will tend to be taken into consideration by investors, and this is another influential factor. The operations of the Federal Reserve likewise play a major role in determining interest rates. The Federal Reserve often buys or sells treasury bills to *ease* or *tighten* the money supply. If the Fed is operating on a large scale, it can have a substantial impact on the level of interest rates.

Treasury bills offer attractive tax benefits for the large investor. Income from them is treated as ordinary taxable income at the federal level, but it is exempt from state and local income taxes. It is important, however, to check with your tax advisor on your own specific tax needs. There are various strategies portfolio managers take advantage of when investing in money market instruments. You may have heard the terms *yield spreads* and *riding the yield curve*. For the most part, however, these concepts are too sophisticated for the individual investor. They are of greater concern to professionals who manage large pools of money.

So far we have learned that treasury bills are direct obligations of the federal government; they are sold on a discount basis in minimum denominations of $10,000; they are quoted in terms of rate of return; they have short maturities ranging up to one year; they are considered safe; and income from them is exempt from state and local—but *not* federal—taxes.

Bankers' Acceptances

Bankers' acceptances are irrevocable obligations of the banks which issue them. They are drafts drawn by banks that promise to honor them at maturity. Bankers' acceptances are created to finance transactions in specific commodities or to facilitate money exchanges with foreign banks.

For example, let us suppose that an American company wanted to import widgets from an exporter in Transylvania. The importer might ask his bank to issue a letter of credit in favor of the Transylvanian exporter. This letter contains all the details of the transaction: shipment, terms of the agreement, and the amount for which the exporter may draw a time draft on the bank. The importer agrees to pay the bank when shipment has been made and he has received his widgets. While the bank expects to receive payment from the American importer, it is the exporter who remains contingently liable during the life of the transaction. He discounts his draft at his own Transylvanian bank, which has been notified of the agreement by the American bank. The shipping documents and draft are sent by the Transylvanian bank to the American bank, where the draft is stamped "accepted" by an officer. This draft is now an acceptance and, as such, it is an irrevocable obligation of the American bank. Usually, the Transylvanian bank will discount the acceptance with the American bank, which then may sell it to a securities dealer or retain it in its loan portfolio.

If you are thoroughly confused at this point, don't be alarmed. You're not alone. I think it is safe to say that most stockbrokers don't fully understand the ins and outs of this market. Consider yourself ahead of the game if you can grasp the basic concept stated earlier, that these securities are created to facilitate dollar exchanges with foreign banks, or to finance transactions in specific commodities.

The example above is just one of many I could have used. This same deal could have been financed by the American importer instead of the Transylvanian exporter, in which case the widgets would have been shipped to the importer but released to him only when payment had been made. The importer would have drawn a time draft on the American bank. When this draft was accepted by the bank, payment would have been made to the Transylvanian exporter, and the importer would then have been free to sell the widgets. Again, a fairly complicated transaction. Just keep in mind that bankers' acceptances represent irrevocable obligations of the bank.

Besides facilitating transactions with foreign companies, bankers' acceptances are sometimes used to finance shipments of goods between countries, domestic shipments, domestic or foreign storage of readily marketable staples that are secured by an independent warehouse receipt, and dollar exchanges with banks of approved foreign countries.

Maturity periods of bankers' acceptances are shorter than for treasury bills, and range up to 270 days. The interest on them is paid in the form of a discount when they are purchased. This income, however, is subject to federal, state, and local income taxes, and it is generally treated as ordinary income.

Since bankers' acceptances are sold in minimum denominations of $100,000, they are of major concern to institutions with large pools of money to invest for short periods of time. The average investor may have some money invested in them if he buys shares in a money market mutual fund. As such, the bankers' acceptances will be part of an overall money market portfolio. We'll talk about this concept a little more when we get into the section on mutual funds.

To summarize what has been covered so far, bankers' acceptances are irrevocable obligations of the banks that issue them. They are created to finance transactions in specific commodities or to facilitate dollar exchanges with foreign banks. Their maturity periods range up to 270 days. The interest they pay is discounted in the purchase price. And they are sold in minimum amounts of $100,000.

Certificates of Deposit

Certificates of Deposit (CDs for short, and not to be confused with the long-term savings deposits in banks also called "certificates of deposit") are issued by commercial banks, which are constantly searching for funds to supply their lending operations. CDs are obligations of the issuing bank to pay the beneficial holder or bearer the face amount plus interest at maturity. They are usually sold in a coupon form, unlike the discounted treasury bills and bankers' acceptances. When they are issued you pay the face amount and receive the interest at the end. CD maturities range from one month up to one year. Minimum denominations here are $100,000.

Both CDs and bankers' acceptances have historically been extremely safe investments. There is no record of any investor ever having sustained a loss on his principal on a bankers' acceptance issued by an American bank, and CDs are considered to be of similar quality.

Again, this is a market primarily for institutional investors. The banking system raises large sums of money for its own needs by issuing CDs. Institutions sometimes buy them with maturity dates coming when cash is needed to pay taxes, dividends, and other expenses. They also buy them to maintain high *liquidity*, that is, to be able to raise cash for immediate needs while having it earn interest when it is idle for short periods of time. Putting it another way, the banks need money and institutions and large investors have substantial sums. Idle money has to be put to work for short periods. This money is deposited with a commercial bank, channeled into the banking system in the form of short-term time deposits.

To summarize the main features of CDs, they are obligations of commercial banks; they are usually sold in coupon form; they are safe; and the interest they pay is subject to income taxes on all levels.

Commercial Paper

Commercial paper is negotiable short-term promissory notes issued by well-known corporations for any term up to 270 days.

These notes are sold in face amounts of $100,000, $250,000, $500,000, $1,000,000, and combinations of these amounts. Unlike other money market instruments, which are either government or bank securities, commercial paper represents *corporate indebtedness* of nonfinancial private enterprises. Corporations engaged in various fields, including manufacturing, retailing, and transportation, usually use the proceeds from commercial paper to fill their short-term cash needs. As in the case of both treasury bills and bankers' acceptances, commercial paper is discounted.

As you might have expected because of the large dollar amounts involved, investors in commercial paper are primarily banks, insurance companies, mutual funds, pension funds, nonfinancial corporations, and other institutions with large pools of money to invest on a short-term basis.

Standard and Poor and Moody evaluate and rate most of the corporations issuing commercial paper today. The ratings, however, are different from those used for bonds. Standard and Poor's A-1, A-2, and A-3 and Moody's Prime-1, Prime-2, and Prime-3 are most generally acceptable to investors.

The yields on commercial paper are usually the highest among the money market instruments, while treasury bill yields are usually lowest. Although commercial paper is considered safe, it carries more risk than T-bills. The interest rates of all these securities are greatly influenced by the Federal Reserve's moves to loosen or tighten the growth of money and credit. Overall supply and demand for credit are also major factors in determining interest rates, as well as anticipated changes in money and credit growth. As is the case with all money market instruments except treasury bills, the interest they pay is treated as ordinary income subject to federal, state, and local income taxes.

You now know that commercial paper is short-term promissory notes issued by corporations, which mature in periods of up to 270 days. They are sold at a discount and rated for quality. And their interest is taxable.

Miscellaneous

Some schools of thought maintain that long-term debt obligations with *less than a year* remaining until maturity become money market instruments. For example, a 25-year bond due for redemption six months from now is considered by some people to be a money market instrument. This is not a generally accepted view, however, and since trading in these securities is rare, it is more an academic question than anything else.

As I pointed out at the beginning of this chapter, the capital market ties up your money for longer than a year. The capital market is a mechanism for raising long-term capital (the primary market), and for buying and reselling *securities* (the secondary market). The main focus here is the point of view and needs of the institution raising the money. The institution relies on the capital market to satisfy long-term capital needs. The securities sold here range in life from one year to perpetuity.

What are capital market securities? They include common stocks, preferred stocks, and bonds, all of which we have discussed. (The fact that investors can trade in and out of stocks in less than a year is not important. What does matter is that corporations issue stocks to satisfy their long-term financial requirements.) Also included here are long-term loans and mortgages.

A moment ago I mentioned primary and secondary markets. This distinction is easy to understand. The *primary market* is the mechanism by which new issues are originally distributed. When a corporation wants to raise money for long-term needs, it may decide to float a new issue of stocks or bonds. The whole procedure of finding underwriters to sell new issues to the public is done in the primary market. The *secondary market* consists of the exchanges and over-the-counter markets where securities are *resold*. Obviously, no one would buy a stock or a bond if it could not be sold at the investor's discretion. The secondary market provides liquidity, a mechanism for the exchange of securities between buyers and sellers.

This wraps up the main elements in our discussion of money market instruments and the capital market. To summarize, financial markets are divided into the money market and the capital market. The money market instruments are treasury bills, bankers' acceptances, certificates of deposit, and commercial paper, all maturing in one year or less. The capital market ties up money for more than a year, and the securities traded here are stocks, bonds, and other long-term obligations.

As far as buying money market instruments is concerned, there is no physical location such as a stock exchange where they are traded. Trading is done over the phone in a negotiated market. Your broker can give you quotes for different securities with various maturities if you decide to invest in this market.

You now have a basic grasp of the main things you should know about money market instruments, common and preferred stocks, and corporate bonds. Let's move on now to Treasury and government agency securities.

4

What Are Treasury and Government Agency Securities?

Strictly speaking, U.S. government and federal agency securities with maturities of longer than a year are not considered money market instruments. However, these longer-term securities are of great interest to the investor since they are extremely liquid; there is a ready market for them and they can be quickly bought and sold. They are also regarded to be safe investments, another important criterion. Our purpose in this chapter is to familiarize ourselves with the various kinds of government agency securities and Treasury bonds and notes which are available for the short-, intermediate-, and long-term investor.

Again, I would like to point out that the world of financial investments seems complicated and confusing because of the broad variety of securities on the market. Our object here is not to memorize all these definitions as though we were being tested for a school assignment, but gradually to build up a familiarity with these vehicles. If you can, put aside the questions that are probably foremost in your mind now—"How can I possibly choose from all these investments?" or "How can I possibly know which ones would be right for me?" When we finish with part one, "Understanding Securities," and get into part two, "How to Invest," these questions will not seem as difficult to answer as they might right now.

For now, let's just stick to trying to become as familiar with securities as we can, turning now to Treasury bonds and notes and the various federal agency securities.

Treasury Notes and Bonds

Treasury bills, you may remember, are obligations of the U.S. government maturing in periods of from three months to one year. *Treasury notes* are issued to provide the federal government with medium-term funds to finance the public debt. Traditionally, the maturities on notes have been from one to seven years, although recently this definition has been extended to cover ten-year obligations. *Treasury bonds* are issued to provide the federal government with long-term funds to finance the public debt, and their maturity periods have traditionally been from seven to thirty years. Again, this definition has been changed to include some obligations of less than seven years. From this we can see that, in terms of maturity, the distinction between a note and a bond is not always precise. Since this gray area does exist, it is enough to keep the main concept in mind, which can be stated as:

Treasury bills: Short-term
Treasury notes: Medium-term
Treasury bonds: Long-term

Currently, both notes and bonds are available in denominations ranging from $1000 to $1,000,000. Treasury notes are usually sold in bearer form (not registered in the name of the purchaser), while bonds are issued in either bearer or registered form. Unlike treasury bills, neither the bonds nor the notes are sold at discount since their maturity periods are longer. You buy them at face value (or market value after they are issued), and the interest is ordinarily paid semiannually. This interest, as in the case of bills, is exempt from state and local income taxes, but not federal taxes.

This is enough about treasury notes and bonds for our purposes here. Notes are medium-term obligations of the U.S. government; bonds are long-term obligations. They are ordinarily available in denominations as low as $1000. Treasury notes are usually sold in bearer form, and the bonds in either bearer or registered form. Interest is exempt from state and local income taxes and it is paid twice a year.

Series E and H Bonds

Other types of guaranteed debt securities issued by the federal government are U.S. Treasury Series E and Series H bonds. These are savings bonds and they are not marketable. They are registered in the owner's name and are not transferable to other parties. You can buy them at authorized outlets, primarily banks and post offices.

Series E bonds are issued in denominations ranging from $25 to $1000, and the interest is paid in the form of a discount; that is, you buy them at a discount of 25 percent from face value and you redeem them in ten years at slightly more than face value, depending on the promised interest yield. If you decide to redeem them before the ten-year period, there is a yield penalty. Series E bonds offer safety of principal, an exemption from state income taxes, and a deferral on paying federal income taxes until you redeem the bonds if you so choose. And E bonds can be used to buy Series H bonds.

Series H bonds are similar to E bonds except for two main

58

features: you buy Series H bonds at face value, and your interest is paid to you semiannually. Like E bonds, they can be redeemed prior to maturity with a one month's written notice. There is also a yield penalty for early redemption.

Government Agency Securities

There are several major issuers of government agency securities: federal intermediate credit banks; banks for cooperatives; federal land banks; federal home loan banks; and the Federal National Mortgage Association. These are of more interest to those in the institutional investment market, although some individual investors are attracted to them as well. They usually offer higher yields than securities issued by the U.S. Treasury, yet they are very safe. In addition, trading in these securities is active because of the institutional activity, so the liquidity is high (that is, both new and old issues can be bought and sold with ease).

Taking them one by one, federal intermediate credit banks provide short-term and medium-term credit for the agricultural industry. These banks make loans to production credit associations, which, in turn, make loans to farmers. To raise money for these lending operations, the banks issue consolidated bonds for which they are jointly and severally liable. These bonds, it should be noted, are *not* obligations of the U.S. government, which accounts for their normally having higher yields than Treasury securities. Minimum denominations are $5000, and maturities are usually nine months, but occasionally longer.

Banks for cooperatives are a somewhat smaller source of short- and medium-term credit for the agricultural industry. These banks, together with the Central Bank for Farmers' Cooperatives, are engaged in various aspects of marketing agricultural products. They likewise raise funds through the sale of consolidated bonds, which are not obligations of the federal government. (The ownership of these banks rests with various farmers' cooperatives in the form of common stock.) The co-ops (as these bonds are sometimes called) are normally issued with maturities of six months, and they are sold in minimum denominations of $5000.

Federal land banks supply long-term credit to farmers through federal land bank associations for capital expenditures on livestock, land, farm machinery, etc. Money is raised by the land banks through the sale of consolidated bonds, which are issued through a fiscal agent who uses the marketing services of various dealers. Although the maturities of these securities are frequently for longer periods than those of the first two agency securities we mentioned, they have an active market, are highly liquid, and they can be bought in denominations of $1000.

The function of the federal home loan banks is to serve as a reserve credit agency for member savings and loan associations and other thrift institutions that make home mortgage loans. These banks make loans to their member institutions. To raise money for these loans, they issue bonds called joint consolidated obligations. These home loans are not obligations of the U.S. government. Maturity periods are available for both short and longer terms, and the minimum denomination is $10,000.

The Federal National Mortgage Association, or Fannie Mae, was created to give supplementary assistance for federally guaranteed and insured mortgages. Today Fannie Mae is set up as a privately owned instrumentality of the United States, similar in status to the federal land and federal home loan banks. Fannie Mae buys mortgages that are insured or guaranteed by the Federal Housing Administration (FHA), the Veterans Administration (VA), and the Farmers Home Administration (FHA) from various financial institutions (for example, life insurance companies and savings and loan associations), and then resells them at various times. Fannie Mae is a corporation, and it has issued debentures and common stock which are traded on major exchanges. These debentures are not obligations of the government, and are issued with varying maturity periods, ranging from short-term to as long as twenty-five years. Fannie Mae has also issued short-term discount notes similar to commercial paper. (All the other federal agencies mentioned here issue discount notes too.)

Income on most agency securities is exempt from state and local income taxes. For specific questions it is best to consult a tax advisor.

Ginnie Maes

I have decided to talk to you about Ginnie Maes separately and at some length because they are of more interest to the individual investor than are the other government agency securities discussed above. As far as the latter go, it is enough for you to have a passing acquaintance with them. Chances are you will have little if anything to do with them when setting up your own individual portfolio.

Ginnie Maes, however, fall into a different category. They are, first of all, fully guaranteed government securities. The term Ginnie Mae is actually a nickname for the Government National Mortgage Association (GNMA), which has the responsibility of owning, controlling, and managing the assets of Fannie Mae. The most unique and popular of the securities which GNMA guarantees are called pass-throughs, and it is these we will talk about here.

A *Ginnie Mae certificate* represents a share in a pool of government-guaranteed mortgages. A mortgage banker might assemble a package of mortgages, most frequently on single-family homes, although some are on FHA project loans such as apartments and hospitals, and then place them in the custody of a commercial bank. Ginnie Mae then issues a *pass-through security*, which is collateralized by the mortgages in the package. This security, by the way, is called a pass-through because the mortgage payments made by the home buyer or other mortgagee are passed through to the investor. Since these mortgage payments are made on a monthly basis, the investors in Ginnie Maes receive monthly checks, which makes these securities an attractive investment vehicle. Each month the investor receives a proportionate share of all principal and interest from the mortgages in the pool.

Ginnie Mae guarantees that the investor will receive prompt payment of principal and interest even if the mortgagees do not pay on time. In addition, all scheduled payments of principal and interest are relatively uniform for the life of the certificate. In the event of any prepayments of mortgages in the pool, the monthly payments are supplemented proportionately. Since World War II, the average life of most single-family mortgage packages has been about twelve years, primarily because of prepaid mortgages. As prepayments occur, the Ginnie Mae investor's principal is returned along with interest.

The minimum denomination for Ginnie Mae pass-throughs is $25,000, with increments of $5000 above this figure.

Tables are available indicating the approximate initial monthly payment for Ginnie Mae investors at various interest rates. Depending on current market prices, for example, it is possible to determine how much you can expect to get in interest and principal for the amount of money you are investing in a particular Ginnie Mae. Payments are accompanied by a monthly remittance statement showing the breakdown in interest, principal, and prepayments to facilitate bookkeeping.

Generally speaking, the yields on Ginnie Maes have been the best among all government securities, and at times they have been competitive with corporate bonds, which are not considered to be as safe as Ginnie Maes. They can be easily bought and sold since there is an active market for them. The interest they pay is treated as ordinary income that is not exempt from federal, state, or local income taxes. Finally, they are sold only in registered form.

In this chapter we have discussed treasury notes and bonds, and the various types of government agency securities. We have also learned that Ginnie Mae pass-throughs are fully guaranteed government securities combining the best features of mortgages and government bonds. They offer safety and payments in the form of monthly checks. Their average life is twelve years and you need a minimum of $25,000 to buy them.

From "governments," let's now turn our attention to mutual funds.

5

What Are Mutual Funds and Other Investment Companies?

Mutual Funds

A *mutual fund* is a type of investment company. The purpose of mutual funds is to allow smaller investors to pool their investment dollars and benefit from professional management techniques that are usually available only to wealthy individuals and institutions. One of the major attractions of mutual funds to the inexperienced investor is that his money is managed by a professional. It is a convenient means of contracting the investment decision-making process to someone else.

A mutual fund is the most common type of investment company (we will talk about some of the others later). It is established as a corporation or a trust that issues securities. The funds from the sale of these securities are invested in a diversified portfolio that is selected and managed by professionals. The major distinction between a mutual fund and other financial institutions is that a mutual fund's main function and only objective, required by law, must be the professional management of investment money. It cannot be a mere adjunct to other activities. For example, banks and insurance companies also invest pools of money, but this is not their main activity.

The kind of securities that a mutual fund invests in will depend on the stated objectives of the fund. In the section on money market instruments I mentioned that it is possible for small investors to buy shares in a money market fund (also called a "ready assets" or "liquid assets" fund). In this case, your individual money would be pooled and invested in a portfolio consisting exclusively of treasury bills, CDs, and other short-term instruments. Likewise, an income fund might contain corporate bonds, preferred stocks, and other securities offering high yields; a growth fund might invest in common stock of corporations in different industries providing an opportunity for capital appreciation; and it is possible to buy shares in a mutual fund offering a combination of financial objectives.

A mutual fund is also called an *open-end company*. This means that, after the initial public offering is made, additional shares are offered for sale to the public indefinitely. By law, the only kind of security that can be issued by mutual funds or other open-end companies is voting common stock. When you invest your money in a mutual fund you are actually buying shares of ownership in the form of common stock. These shares may be listed on an exchange or they may be traded over the counter.

The prices of mutual fund shares are calculated daily by the net value of the fund's portfolio. From this we can see that the value of the shares is directly related to the performance of the securities in the portfolio. Consequently, just how well or how poorly the professional managers of each fund are doing can be seen each day in the market value of the shares. The net asset value (NAV) per share is calculated by dividing the fund's net assets by the number of shares outstanding. This NAV is usually quoted in the newspapers as the *bid price*—the price you will get if you want to sell your shares. The *offer price* is what you have to pay if you want to buy shares in a mutual fund. The offer price is normally the NAV plus a sales charge, or load, if there is one. The offer price will ordinarily be higher than the NAV to reflect the load, or the same as NAV if it is a *no-load* (no-sales-charge) fund. The sales charge in a load fund is currently stated as a percentage of the net asset value per share.

If you invest in a mutual fund, you will find that there usually are several types of investment plans available. Most of them offer a variety of periodic payment plans for investors who want to invest money on a systematic basis. Many funds offer to redeem your shares without extra charges, and they offer conversion privileges within a family of funds if your objectives should change—that is, they offer the possibility of converting from a growth fund to an income fund at the investor's discretion. Also, some funds have programs for automatic reinvestment of dividends and other distributions, capital withdrawal, and other provisions that are explained in each fund's prospectus.

If you purchase shares in a mutual fund by buying a specific number of shares, or by contracting to invest a specific amount of money, you will most likely receive whole shares plus a fraction of a share. In other words, you can buy 50, 100, or 200 shares, or you can invest a fixed sum, say $3000, and receive as many shares to the fraction that it will buy. When you buy into a load fund, in most cases the sales charge percentage is scaled down for larger purchases. The sales charge schedule will show you the various breakpoints, the dollar figures necessary to get reduced sales charges. For example, purchases of under $25,000 might carry a 9 percent charge; $25,000 but less than $50,000, a 6 percent load, $50,000 but less than $100,000, a 4 percent load, etc.

Reduction in a mutual fund's sales charge or load can also be obtained by signing a *letter of intent*. If you intended to invest $50,000, using our example above, but only have $35,000 available now, you could agree to invest the full amount over a period not to exceed thirteen months and qualify for the lower load. Many mutual funds also offer their shareholders the *right of accumulation*, which means you would have the right to include your total investment in the fund to date as a base for determining future sales charges. It is important to read a fund's prospectus carefully to find out exactly what you are entitled to. By law, you must be informed of the existence of breakpoints beforehand so you can take advantage of reduced loads.

As far as the types of accumulation plans are concerned, they fall into three basic categories: voluntary accumulation, periodic payment, and variable annuity. If you should ever decide to invest in a mutual fund, the salesman can explain in detail how these plans work. For our purposes here, it is enough for you to have a general idea of what's involved. The *voluntary accumulation plan* allows you to invest varying amounts of money at your convenience. This plan gives you the most flexibility. A *periodic payment plan* is a more formal contract under which you agree to invest a fixed sum of money at set intervals over a specified period. (These plans are frequently called *front-end-load* plans since most of the total sales charges are deducted "up front" from the earlier payments. A *spread load* option entitles you to spread the sales charge over a longer period of time, although it is still basically a front-end load.) The third plan mentioned a moment ago, the variable annuity, is a retirement plan sold by insurance companies. This provides the investor with a lifelong income, usually upon retirement. The amounts you receive depend upon how well the portfolio of securities that you invested in performed throughout the life of the contract.

The rules and regulations governing rights of withdrawal are extremely complex. If you, the investor, should decide to pull out of one of these programs anywhere along the way, the amount of money you will actually get back and the amount you will have to *surrender* (that is, give up in the form of a penalty) are determined beforehand by various formulas. Just be sure you understand exactly what the terms of the contract call for before signing anything. Don't tie yourself to any plan or system of payments unless you know exactly what you are doing.

Summing up what we have discussed about mutual funds, we know that they are a type of investment company. They offer you the opportunity to invest your money (buy shares) in a professionally managed portfolio of securities. These securities can be stocks, bonds, money market instruments, or any combination of securities depending on the stated objectives of the fund. Mutual funds may carry a sales charge, or load, or they may be no-load. The bid and offer price of each fund depends upon the performance of the securities in the portfolio, and they are quoted in most major newspapers. They offer a wide variety of investment plans, reinvestment plans, and redemption and conversion privileges. Because of the many types of funds that are available, it is important to understand exactly what you are contracting for if you should decide to invest in one.

Unit Investment Trusts

A *unit investment trust* does not issue stock or debt securities. Securities in a unit investment trust consist of shares, or units, of *beneficial interest* (SBI), which represent an interest in a portfolio of securities owned by the trust.

Unit investment trusts may be either fixed trusts or participating trusts. In a *fixed trust*, the number of SBI and the portfolio of securities remain the same throughout the life of the trust. If a trust offers 50,000 units to the public initially, it does not issue new units later on. This number is fixed. (Remember that a mutual fund is continually offering new shares.) And once the portfolio is set up, it remains unchanged. It is not a traded or managed portfolio as in the case of a mutual fund. Municipal bond and corporate income trusts are popular forms of unit investment trusts. In these trusts, bonds are selected for the portfolio and usually remain there until maturity unless they are called before then. Each unit represents a proportionate share of interest in each bond. Each unit costs approximately $1000, and the investor receives interest payments in the form, ordinarily, of monthly checks. The firms sponsoring these trusts generally maintain a secondary OTC market for the units so they can be bought and sold on a continuing basis, although underwriting firms are not obligated to do so.

A *participating trust* issues shares in a specific investment company other than the trust. In effect, it acts as a middleman. It is limited to purchasing only one security with its investors' money. Sometimes, shares in a mutual fund are marketed through a participating trust.

Face Amount Certificate Companies

A *face-amount certificate company* (FAC), like mutual funds and unit investment trusts, is a kind of investment company. An FAC issues debt securities and pays the investor a fixed rate of interest. It may invest in U.S. government and municipal obligations, prime real estate and mortgages, and investment-grade stocks, and it normally guarantees the investor a minimum interest rate. You usually buy these certificates in installments on a discount basis (for less than the face amount which will be paid at maturity). FACs are so simliar to annuities sold by insurance companies that in some states they are regulated and supervised by state insurance commissioners.

Miscellaneous

As we saw earlier, a mutual fund is an open-end company. A *closed-end management company* usually raises capital for investment through a one-time public offering of shares. Occasionally, however, it may issue bonds, preferred stock, warrants, or even more common stock with the consent of its present shareholders. (A mutual fund, or open-end company, may issue only voting common stock, as you may recall, and additional shares are issued continually.) Also, after the initial public offering is made, the shares in a closed-end company are traded on an exchange or OTC just like common stock in any corporation. Market value of these shares is determined by supply and demand; it is not tied to NAV. Nor are the shares redeemed on a regular basis. From this we can see that a closed-end company is very similar to any other corporation except that it is set up as a management company; its sole objective is to invest capital in specific areas.

Wrapping up this chapter, you have learned that there are several types of investment companies. There are management companies, unit investment trusts, and face-amount certificate companies. Management companies can be either closed-end or open-end. If they are closed-end, the securities they issue are traded on exchanges or OTC just like the securities of any other corporation. Open-end companies are called mutual funds, and they issue only common stock, on a continuous basis.

Later on, we will talk about how all these investments might fit into your overall financial strategy. But for now, let's continue with our familiarization with basic elements, turning to a subject close to the hearts of most of us in this age of higher and higher taxes: tax-free income.

6

What Is a Municipal Bond?

Tax-free income has become more and more popular with an increasing number of people over the years. At one time this type of investment was considered to be a vehicle exclusively for the rich. Today, with inflation and rising nominal incomes, more people are suddenly finding themselves in tax brackets that make tax-free income an important consideration for them. More women are entering the work force, providing families with a second paycheck, and it is not difficult these days for a husband and wife to discover that they are in a 30, 35, or 40 percent tax bracket.

A tax-free investment can provide an exemption from federal and, in some cases, state and local income taxes. The most common tax-free investments are *municipal bonds*. These bonds are issued by states, counties, cities, and other local governments, and by the various special-purpose legal agencies and authorities of these governments.

The most important consideration for you, the investor, is that the interst paid by municipal debt securities is exempt from federal, and sometimes from state and local, income taxes. What this means in terms of dollars is higher *net income*. If someone is in a 40 percent income-tax bracket, a municipal bond (sometimes called a "muni") yield of 6 percent is equivalent to a 10 percent yield from a corporate bond. (A corporate bond yielding $100 per $1000, or 10 percent, taxable at a rate of 40 percent, will provide you with a *net* of $60, or 6 percent, after taxes.) From this we can see that the higher your tax bracket, the more important tax-free income is to you. In the example above, if you were in a 50 percent bracket, you would need a yield of 12 percent from a corporate bond or stock in order to net the 6 percent the muni would give you. If you were in a 25 percent income tax bracket you would need an equivalent yield of 8 percent to net 6 percent.

Your broker has a chart showing equivalent yields for each tax bracket, but you can figure it out yourself by dividing the muni yield by the correlative of your tax bracket. If you are in a 40 percent bracket, to figure out the equivalent yield on a 6 percent municipal bond you merely divide 6 percent or 0.06 by 0.60 and you get 0.10, or 10 percent. At the 25 percent bracket, you divide 6 percent by 0.75 since 75 percent is the correlative of 25 percent. I hope this isn't too confusing. It all became clearer to me after I worked the figures a few times and understood the basic concept. To simplify things, you can always ask your broker for a conversion chart.

Before you decide to invest in a muni, you have to figure out what you need in terms of taxable income to give you the same net income you will get from the tax-free bond. If you are in a 40 percent bracket and need 10 percent to net 6 percent, you then want to find out if you can get 10 percent or better from a different investment that is also reasonably safe. If you can get better than 10 percent from a good-quality taxable investment, you might be better off investing in that instead of the 6 percent muni. If, after looking around, you find out you cannot do better than 8.5 percent, the 6 percent municipal bond may look more attractive to you. In other words, you want to find out where your break-even point is. (I realize we are beginning to touch on investment strategy here, but it is hard to avoid it when discussing tax-free investments.)

As a general rule, when you buy bonds issued outside the state you live in, the interest will be exempt from federal income tax, but you will have to pay state and local income taxes on it. If you buy munis issued inside the state you live in, your exemption will apply at both the federal and state level. And if you live in New York City and buy New York City bonds, you will have a triple exemption, from federal, state, and city taxes. This is, as I said, a general guide. Before you buy munis, you should find out exactly what your tax-free status will be. Two exceptions to the general rule are bonds issued by the Commonwealth of Puerto Rico and the District of Columbia, which are exempt from *all* federal and state income taxes.

Historically, municipal bonds have been considered second only to U.S. government bonds as far as safety is concerned. The problems in New York City, Yonkers, and other municipalities throughout the country have made many investors wary of municipal debt instruments, especially those issued by the larger cities. It remains to be seen whether or not the politicians will take the necessary steps to put their financial houses in order on a long-range basis. Investors requiring the tax benefits provided by municipal bonds are well advised to select their issues cautiously.

Ratings

Like corporate bonds, munis are rated to give you an idea of their relative safety. Standard and Poor, Moody, and Fitch base their ratings on the bond issuer's past performance in paying interest and principal and on its *current* and estimated future ability to do so.

The rating symbols are the same as for corporate bonds.

Standard and Poor and Fitch rank municipal bonds as follows: AAA—prime, AA—high grade, A—upper medium grade, BBB —lower medium grade, B—various degrees of risk; anything below this is considered marginal.

Moody's symbols are: Aaa—best quality, Aa—high quality, A—higher medium grade, Baa—lower medium grade, Ba— speculative elements, B—lacking desirable characteristics; anything below this is poor to highly speculative.

In rating munis, the services take into consideration the current economic condition of the issuing municipality or agency, its unemployment rate, its new business and bankruptcy statistics, its retail sales per capita, and other indicators in order to determine the issuer's ability to meet its debt obligations. A municipal bond with one of the four top ratings is considered secure enough by law for investment by *fiduciaries* (those responsible for investing other people's money). There are legal lists available describing the kinds of investments fiduciaries can invest in.

Bearer and Registered Bonds

When you buy municipal bonds, you can buy them in either bearer or registered form. If they are registered, the name of the owner is registered in the records of the municipality and interest is usually sent directly to the registered owner.

Most people, however, prefer to buy these bonds in *bearer* form. They are delivered to the buyer without his name appearing on the records or on the bond certificate, and they come with coupons attached. You receive interest by clipping the appropriate coupon and presenting it for payment on a specific date. Since most people invest in munis because of the tax benefits they offer, they usually do not want their names appearing on any official records.

Buying Munis

As is the case with corporate securities, municipal bonds are offered in both the primary and secondary markets. In the primary market new issues of these bonds are underwritten by investment banking firms and sold to the public. Afterward, municipal bonds are bought and sold in the secondary, or over-the-counter, market through brokerage firms, some banks, and municipal bond dealers. Your broker may work for a firm that makes a market in municipal bonds, in which case he will be able to give you a quote over the phone. Or he will contact a dealer who will give him a quote that he will pass on to you.

Most municipal bonds today are sold in minimum denominations of $5000 and multiples of this figure. However, smaller investors can buy into a municipal bond fund or unit investment trust for less money, usually in multiples of about $1000.

The major benefits of municipal bonds, besides their tax-free status include: safety of principal, liquidity with an active secondary market for them, and diversity, since there are so many different issuers to choose among.

If you should decide to buy munis, you will find that they are divided into several categories. Let's talk about them one by one.

General Obligation Bonds

The *general obligation (GO) bond* is the most common of all munis. This type of bond is backed by the full faith and credit and taxing power of the issuer for payment of interest and principal. As a matter of fact, a statement to this effect is usually printed on the face of the bond certificate itself. General obligation bonds are secured by the taxing power of the issuing governmental unit. The usual source of revenue for city and county GO bonds is real estate taxes, while states normally secure their GO bonds with a combination of income, sales, motor vehicle, tobacco, and liquor taxes. The issuer of a GO bond, in effect, is making a pledge to collect as much tax as necessary to satisfy its obligations to investors in its general obligation bonds.

Special Assessment Bonds

Special assessment bonds are usually issued to finance the construction of specific public facilities, which include streets, curbs, alleys, and sewer systems. Principal and interest are ordinarily payable from tax assessments made against those who benefit from the facilities. In some instances, these bonds may be a form of GO bond if they are backed by the full faith and credit and taxing power of the issuer. If this is the case, they could overlap other GO obligations. This could put a strain on other debt obligations and affect the bond rating.

Revenue Bonds

Revenue bonds are ordinarily issued to finance the construction of public facilities that are expected to produce revenue. Projects such as airport construction, college dormitories, and rapid transit systems are among those financed by these bonds. Revenue bonds are generally issued by a local or state authority; they are not obligations of the locality or state. In most cases, the interest and principal is paid from the revenues produced by the facilities financed by the bonds. For this reason, the rating of revenue bonds is especially important, since the return to the investor depends on the solvency of the particular public facility his money helped build.

Industrial Revenue Bonds

Industrial revenue bonds were issued at one time to finance the construction of factories and industrial parks. These were leased to private corporations, which paid rent to the municipality. In recent years, however, the tax-exempt status of industrial revenue bonds has been curtailed and, as a result, there have not been that many new issues. The old bonds are still traded in the secondary market.

Housing Authority Bonds

Housing authority bonds are usually issued by a public housing authority (PHA) to finance the construction of public housing projects. Federal housing authority (FHA) bonds are secured by revenues from rent and federal-grant subsidies. Because of this tie-in with the federal government, they are backed by the full faith and credit of the United States and are rated AAA. These are the safest of all housing authority bonds. PHA bonds do not have the backing of the federal government and they carry various ratings.

Miscellaneous

You may recall from the section on corporate bonds that serial bonds are issued with different maturity dates, and series bonds have different issue dates but the same maturity date. You should know that the majority of munis are serial bonds. A municipality will usually issue new bonds that mature, one group at a time, over a period of many years. Municipalities sometimes issue bonds with a *balloon maturity*, which means they mature in increasingly larger amounts as the final maturity date draws near. Most bonds with balloon maturities are also callable. In the corporate market, most bonds are *term* bonds issued on one date and all maturing on the same date. Term bonds are rarely issued in the municipal market.

The various types of municipal bonds discussed above are general but not all-inclusive. Many municipalities issue tax anticipation notes (TANs), revenue anticipation notes (RANs), and bank anticipation notes (BANs), with maturity periods of one year or less. Some also issue pollution control bonds (sometimes issued in conjunction with utilities) and other variations that you should be aware of. Your broker will be able to fill you in on the details of the different bonds available.

It is also possible to buy municipal bonds whose obligations are insured by a conglomerate of private insurance companies. *MBIA-backed bonds* are considered to be the most secure among these munis. *MBIA* stands for the Municipal Bond Insurance Association, a consortium of private insurance companies guaranteeing full payment of principal and interest on MBIA-backed bonds.

So far we have covered the world of common and preferred stocks, corporate bonds, money market instruments, treasuries and government agency securities, mutual funds and other investment companies, and municipal bonds. Municipal bonds provide you with an exemption from federal and, in some cases, state and local income taxes. They are rated for quality and usually bought in bearer form. They come in various categories, which include general obligation, special assessment, revenue, and housing authority bonds. Most munis are serial bonds, and some are insured against default.

Having just finished with a discussion of tax-free income, the next logical step for us is to talk about tax shelters. The distinction between tax-free securities and tax shelters is not difficult to grasp. Yet, for some reason, a good many brokers have failed to fully understand the basic differences.

7

What Is a Tax Shelter?

Since the laws on tax shelters are in a continual state of flux, we will deal with this subject in a more general fashion than previous subjects. In the last chapter we talked about tax-free income through municipal bonds. When you invest in municipal bonds (and other securities) you are investing dollars that you have left *after taxes*. After you have finished with the IRS and paid Uncle Sam his pound of flesh (getting heavier all the time), you may then have some money left over that you can put in a savings account or invest in something else. It is these investable after-tax dollars that we have been concentrating on so far.

When we talk about *tax shelters* we are referring to money you can legally put away before taxes in order to reduce or defer your tax bite. If you earn a gross income of $40,000 a year and you can find a way of putting aside, say, $8000 off the top to reduce the tax liability, you are, in effect, *sheltering* your money so the IRS cannot get at it. Generally speaking, the higher your income tax bracket, the more beneficial a tax shelter can be.

The mood in Washington, D.C., lately has been to close or at least to tighten many of the tax shelter programs that have been available over the years, particularly those for affluent investors. There is no guarantee that the rules of today will be in effect a year or two from this writing. So let's start with those that are least likely to be eliminated or tightened in any appreciable fashion, those available to moderate income groups. The trend seems to be to expand and open up new shelters for middle-income wage earners, while tightening loopholes at the upper end of the income scale.

Keogh

The *Keogh* plan is available to self-employed individuals. This shelter permits a self-employed person to invest as much as 15 percent of his annual pretax self-employment income up to a maximum (at this writing) of $7500 a year in a special retirement account. You can open a Keogh account with a bank in a savings plan offering a fixed interest rate; you can do it through a mutual fund; or you can have a self-directed account with a brokerage firm where you pick and choose your own investments, with certain restrictions on the kinds of securities you may invest in. The interest and dividends that accrue in a Keogh account are not taxed until they are withdrawn. The idea is that you will be in a lower tax bracket when you retire, reducing your taxes on the income.

So, to use an example, if you are self-employed, make $50,000 a year, and are in a 50 percent tax bracket, you can elect to put away 15 percent, or $7500, in a Keogh plan and save $3750 in taxes that would have been owed on the $7500. In addition, the $7500 will earn interest and/or dividends that will not be taxed until they are withdrawn.

The way the plan is presently set up, the money must remain in your Keogh account until you are 59½ years of age; you must take your money out before you are 70½ years old.

The only way you can withdraw this money before 59½ without paying a substantial penalty on top of the normal income tax is if you should become totally disabled.

Having reached the 59½ minimum age, you can then elect to take your funds out in several ways. You can take them in a lump sum, in regular installments over a period not to exceed your life expectancy or that of a spouse, in the form of an annuity providing periodic payments, by purchasing U.S. Retirement Bonds, or a combination of these methods. If you are eligible for Keogh and decide to take advantage of it, your broker can provide you with more specific details along with advice on how to invest money.

By the way, a salaried employee or wage-earner who also has self-employment income is eligible for a Keogh plan, but only on his self-employment income. Someone earning a salary of $30,000 per year and another $10,000 a year in a self-employed capacity can shelter 15 percent of the $10,000 in Keogh. (This person can also have an IRA account, which we will discuss in a moment.)

If you employ others in your business, you must set up Keogh plans for those who have worked for you for at least three years and who work a minimum of 1000 hours a year. The percentage of income contributed for employees must equal the percentage you shelter for yourself. For example, let's suppose you earn $50,000 a year as a self-employed consultant and you annually shelter 15 percent of it, or $7500, in Keogh. You employ a full-time secretary at $10,000 a year and she has worked for you for more than three years. You must also put aside 15 percent of her income, or $1500 a year, in a retirement fund for her, paid for by you. If she has worked for you for less than three years, you are not obligated to do this.

A final point that should be mentioned here is that, with both Keogh and IRA (see below), you are given a 45-day grace period after the end of any year to set up a plan for that year. This is designed to give you the opportunity to review your tax situation before making a decision.

IRA

The concept of *individual retirement accounts* is substantially the same as Keogh, the main distinction being that IRA is for salaried employees and wage-earners who are not covered by a pension or retirement program at work. If you are in this category, you can shelter up to 15 percent of your annual income in an IRA account, up to a maximum currently set at $1500 a year. You can also add an extra $250 a year for an unemployed spouse. If you are covered by a retirement plan at work and move to another company that does not have one, you are permitted to roll over the money in the company retirement plan—take the money out in a lump sum and put it all into an IRA account—if you do so within sixty days. If you are contemplating such a move, you should look into this possibility immediately so that you do not forget about it later on and inadvertently allow the time period to elapse.

There has been some talk lately in Washington about increasing the maximum dollar figures you may shelter in both Keogh and IRA. At this writing there has been no word as to what kind of increase, if any, the legislators have in mind. If you decide to take advantage of either one of these plans, your broker can inform you of any changes in the law.

Limited Partnerships

Perhaps the most effective method of sheltering money used by the more affluent investors today is a *limited partnership*. There have been several changes in the rules governing limited partnerships, but the basic concept is still in effect. A limited partnership provides you with a means of going into business and using the deductions reported in the early years to offset your regular income. The business is divided into shares and these are sold to various investors. You can buy shares with pretax dollars and, as a limited partner, your liability is limited to the amount of your investment. In other words, you can lose your entire investment but you are not liable for any additional losses suffered by the business. The role of the limited partners is to put up the start-up capital in return for which they are legally entitled to certain tax benefits. In the past, some of these deals made it possible for the investor to write off two or three times the amount of cash he put up the first year, but the first-year deduction is now limited to 100 percent. For example, someone investing $50,000 was allowed to take $100,000 or more off his gross income in some cases. This can no longer be done.

The day-to-day management and operation of the business is entrusted to the general partner. While the immediate goal of someone buying a limited partnership is a tax deduction, the hope is that the business will eventually prosper, since the profits are passed along to the limited partners. If this happens, not only do you get your tax write-off, but you stand to realize substantial gains as well.

Obviously, these tax shelter deals carry with them varying degrees of risk. Some are highly speculative and others less so. You should understand, however, that the real risk involves only a portion of the money invested since a sizable chunk of it would have gone in taxes anyway. If you are in a 50 percent tax bracket and invest $50,000, you are actually risking only half of it. Uncle Sam would have taken $25,000 anyway, had the money not been invested.

The types of limited partnerships currently available include oil and gas drilling ventures, real estate investments, equipment leasing, and other programs. They all have minimum initial investment requirements, ranging from several thousand dollars to much higher figures. There is no point in going into any details on these programs since each venture that comes along is tailor-made for each occasion.

If you are in a very high tax bracket and have sufficient wherewithal to consider one of these tax shelters, you should talk to your tax man first and deal with a reputable brokerage firm. The better-known firms won't get involved in a tax shelter program unless it has been checked out thoroughly beforehand. The element of risk is always there, but you can at least take steps to minimize it as much as possible.

Miscellaneous

Other kinds of tax-related investments are available, but many are, strictly speaking, not real shelters since they involve after-tax investment dollars. There are retirement plans established by companies, profit-sharing plans, custodian accounts for children, charitable remainder trusts, annuities, and others of a similar nature.

You should also understand the distinction between tax-*free* income (for example, municipal bonds), tax *shelters* (pretax dollars), and tax-*deferred* income. Tax-deferred income is income from money invested in such a way that you put off paying taxes on it until some *future date* when you are, presumably, in a lower tax bracket. A Keogh plan is a shelter since you are investing pretax dollars, but the income your money earns in a Keogh account is tax-deferred since you pay tax on it when you take it out. Dividends from some utility stocks are sometimes wholly or partially tax-deferred since you may not have to pay taxes on them until you sell the stock (and then the tax you pay is in the form of a larger capital gain taxed at a lower rate than ordinary income). We'll cover this a bit more thoroughly in part two.

That's about all you have to know about tax shelters for our purposes here. A tax shelter is a way of investing money before taxes to reduce your tax bite. Shelters include Keogh, IRA, and various limited partnerships. You are now familiar with the distinctions among tax shelters, tax-free, and tax-deferred income.

8

What Is an Option?

We are now getting into the home stretch in our discussion of securities. Deliberately, I have saved one of the more complicated areas until now. I'm not going to pretend to you that securities options are simple and easy to understand. It took me a solid six months of working in the business before I began to feel comfortable discussing options with any of my clients. I don't think I'm being unkind when I tell you that most brokers—and I do mean a majority—do not fully understand the workings of the options market. This is not their fault particularly. Years ago, options were traded exclusively in the OTC market, and the volume of trading was very low. Listed-options trading on major exchanges is a relatively new phenomenon. As such, it is a constantly evolving field with changes taking place almost every day. It can be complicated and difficult, and there is no short cut to learning the market. This does not mean, however, that you can't grasp the basics of what options are in a reasonably short period of time. The fundamentals are not all that complex, and that is exactly what we are going to talk about in this chapter. The big problem is learning to get a feel for the behavior of options, particularly as they affect certain exotic investment strategies. But that's not a subject for this book. Right now, let's take the basics, one step at a time.

Calls

There are two types of securities options: puts and calls. We'll talk about calls first.

When you buy a *call* you are buying the right to purchase 100 shares of a specific stock at a specific price before a specific date. For example, let's suppose that Polaroid is currently selling at $34 a share. You feel that the stock will move up past 35 within the next three months. On April 2 you buy a Polar-, oid July 35. In this case, Polaroid is the *underlying stock;* 35 is the *strike price;* the particular day in July when the option expires is the *expiration date.* Remember these three terms; they are used constantly in options trading. The period from April 2, when you buy the option, to the expiration date is the *option life.*

In the example above you have until the expiration date to make a move. If Polaroid moves up past 35 to, say, 38, you can buy 100 shares of Polaroid at the strike price, 35, and resell them immediately at the market price for a profit. Or you can sell your option, which will also have gone up in value. In reality, most people who buy options elect to sell them at a profit if they can rather than buy the underlying stock. The reason for this is that they are looking for *leverage.* Options are relatively inexpensive compared to stocks. In our example, you might have paid two points ($200) for the option. (Note that when we are discussing stocks a point is one dollar. But in the case of options, a point is equal to $100.) If Polaroid makes 38 the option could be worth four points ($400), in which case you would have *doubled* your money. If you buy the stock itself for $3500 (100 shares at $35 each) and resell it for $3800, the profit is $300, or less than 10 percent of the investment. If you had bought ten Polaroid July 35s, the investment would have been $2000 and the profit $2000. Since ten options gives you the right to buy 1000 shares (100 shares per option), you would have to lay out $35,000 to make $3000 if you bought and sold the stock. So you can see why most individuals who buy options do not actually buy the underlying stock. By buying and selling the call options themselves, they are getting good leverage for relatively small amounts of money.

Let's pause a moment and review briefly what we've learned about calls so far. The reason for buying a call—or five or ten calls—is that you think the underlying stock will go up within a set period of time. If the stock does indeed go up past the strike price before the expiration date, you could realize a handsome return on your investment by selling your call(s). You can make 50, 100, 200 percent, or more on your money in a few months or less. Sounds terrific so far, right? Where else can you get that kind of leverage? It's like finding a good two-dollar stock and watching it go to five dollars a month or so later. Before you go running out to plunk some money down on call options, however, let's take a look at the other side of the coin.

The other side of the coin is that the underlying stock may not go up at all. Or it may not go up far enough. Or fast enough. Again using our Polaroid July 35s as an example, Polaroid may remain at 34 or it could go down. Then again, it may only go up to 34½, or it may not go up past 35 until August. What happens then? If Polaroid does not go up far or fast enough, or if it goes down, your call option will decline in value. As you approach the expiration date, time literally begins to run out on you. Remember, you have to make your price within a *set period* of time. If you do not, then your calls will *expire worthless* on the expiration date. So, while you have good leverage and can double or triple your money in a short period, you can also lose your entire investment if the underlying stock does not behave the way you want it to.

Until now we have been talking about the buyer of call options. The buyer of options is a *speculator*. This is a high risk investment. But for every buyer there is a seller. Who is actually selling options?

First, the terminology. The seller of call options is also called the *writer*. Just remember that writing calls means the same thing as selling them. Now let's suppose that you own 500 shares of Polaroid. Using the same example, Polaroid is selling for $34 a share on April 2. You decide you would like to increase your income from the stock, so you write five Polaroid July 35s (one for each 100 shares). We mentioned a minute ago that the option was worth two points, or $200, which means you will receive $1000. This return, which might be considered extra dividends, represents almost 6 percent for roughly four months, April through July. The money you receive for writing, or selling, the options is also called your premium, and it is usually more than the stock dividend.

Now let's look at some scenarios. If your stock goes up past 35 by the expiration date, it will be called away from you. Remember, you are obligated to sell it at 35. Assuming you bought it at 34, you would have realized $1000 in options premiums plus a one-point profit in the stock ($1 per share), or another $500, for an 8.9 percent return on your money for a little under four months. Five hundred shares of a $34 stock cost you $17,000. A cash flow of $1500 equals 8.9 percent. Not bad. It is worthwhile noting that, in most cases, your stock will not be called away until the final week before the expiration date. Usually, the only way it could be called away earlier is if the stock were to be well into the money, that is, well above 35, the strike price. (In the above calculations I did not include any dividends you might have received during this period, nor did I include the cost of broker's commissions.)

If, on the other hand, your stock remains at 34 it will not be called away. The buyer loses and you get to keep your stock. You will have received your $1000 in premiums and you can write new options for October. You made roughly 6 percent on your money from April through July, and you can bring in more money for the next three-month period. If your stock declines to 32, you are roughly even. You received two points for the options and you lost two points (on paper, since it is not a real loss until you sell the stock). You have protected yourself two points on the *downside* by writing the options. You can still write new options and keep a cash flow coming in as long as you hang on to the stock.

So far you have learned that buying options is a *high risk* investment while writing them is fairly conservative. The purpose of writing options is to bring in extra income in addition to your dividends and to protect yourself on the downside. When you write options you have to be willing to give up any large profits from any dramatic increase in your stock's price. For example, if Polaroid should move from 34 to 43 before the expiration date, you still have to sell it for 35. This is perhaps the most difficult fact for writers of call options to accept. You have to keep your original intention in mind. Your goal in writing options is cash flow. You have to forget about making huge profits. Some investors who get involved in an ongoing options writing program will just keep buying new stocks when their old ones are called away and continue writing options for that steady cash flow. They are interested in total return rather than quick spurts in the price movements of the underlying stocks.

Puts

Puts are the opposite side of the options coin. When you buy a put you are buying the right to sell 100 shares of a specific stock at a specific price before a specific date. You buy puts in anticipation of lower prices in the underlying stock. So, if Polaroid were selling at 37 and you thought it would fall below 35 by July, you might buy one or five or ten Polaroid July 35 puts. If Polaroid falls, say, to 32 before the expiration date, your puts will be worth more and you can sell them for a profit. Or, perhaps you own a few hundred shares of Polaroid and want to protect yourself against a further decline in the stock. So you buy the July 35s, which give you the right to sell the stock at 35 if it should fall below that. Of course, if Polaroid does not fall below the strike price, 35, within the specified period, your puts will expire worthless. You might also buy puts to lock in a long-term profit. Perhaps you bought a stock at 20 and watched it go up to 50. You could buy puts at 40 to lock in a 20 point profit if the stock should fall back.

The seller, or writer, of put options is agreeing to buy the underlying stock at the strike price if it should fall below that level before the expiration date. If you sold, or wrote, the Polaroid July 35s when Polaroid was at 37, you would have to buy the stock for $35 a share (even if Polaroid falls lower) if the buyer decides to exercise his put, that is, if he decides to take advantage of his right to sell, or put, the stock to you. Normally, you can expect the option to be exercised if the underlying stock is below the strike price during the final week of trading. If Polaroid should remain above 35 for the life of the option, you will have brought in the option premium and not have to buy the stock. You will have speculated and won.

Miscellaneous

What we have discussed so far are the fundamentals of puts and calls. In reality, the world of options trading can be extremely complex. Our purpose in this book is to become familiar with the basics of securities investments. You should not even contemplate buying or writing options until you thoroughly understand the different kinds of investments available and the types of investment strategies people utilize in an effort to make money. Later we will talk a bit about selling short, hedging, and other techniques sometimes related to options trading.

Other terms that you may have heard, but which are beyond our purposes here, are straddles, strips, straps, bull spreads, bear spreads, butterfly spreads, and a host of exotica that you should put aside until you fully understand the material in this book. When you feel that you are ready for more advanced reading, there are books dealing exclusively with options and investment techniques that you can turn to. For the moment it is enough to know that there are two types of securities options: puts and calls. Options are listed on exchanges, and you can follow their price movements from day to day. You buy or write options on an underlying stock with a fixed strike price and a specific expiration date. The present rule is that options expire on the Saturday following the third Friday of the expiration month. Trading in them stops on the preceding business day.

We have come to the end of our discussion of the various types of investment securities. You have learned the difference between debt and equity securities, and we've talked about the various issues in each category. If you like, take some time to review what we've covered so far before moving on. When you're ready, we'll go ahead and talk about what to do when you're actually ready to invest.

Part Two:

How to Invest

9

Picking a Brokerage Firm

Now you understand the basic distinction between a stock and a bond, a common stock and a preferred stock, a corporate bond and a municipal bond, a money market instrument and a capital market security, a mutual fund and a unit investment trust, etc. You have some money in the bank that you feel is not working hard enough for you. You think you can do better by investing it elsewhere.

What do you do next?

Well, the first thing to do is find a brokerage firm. The firm should be conveniently located, which means somewhere close to home or near the place where you work. So you check the yellow pages and find a number of firms that suit the first criterion; they are nearby. Next, which one should you pick from the five or ten listed in the phone book?

In addition to dealing with a brokerage house that is conveniently located, you also want to be sure that the one you pick is (1) reputable, with an established track record for honest, efficient, and reliable service, (2) likely to be in existence five or ten years from now, and (3) able to offer a wide range of services.

Preferably, you want a firm that can handle most, if not all, of your financial needs, not just stock transactions. For these reasons it is probably better to narrow the list to those firms that are widely known. Many small firms offer commission discounts on stock transactions in an effort to establish a clientele. For the most part, however, they do not meet all the criteria outlined above. The better-known firms will be able to help you with the entire range of securities we have talked about. They usually have better research and service facilities, and some have interest-bearing checking accounts via a money market fund. And many have also entered the insurance business with retirement annuities. If you can take care of most of your financial business in one place, you can save yourself a lot of unnecessary walking and bookkeeping. However, if you plan to direct your own investments and do not require the research and backup services of a brokerage firm, you may prefer to take advantage of the commission discounts offered by the discount houses. (For more about brokers' commissions, see pages 113–15 and 145.)

Selecting a Broker

Once the list has been narrowed, the next step is to visit each brokerage firm and pick one for yourself. A list of three is large enough to work with; anything more becomes too time consuming, while a visit to one or two firms may not be enough to give you a chance to make a reasonable decision.

Pick a time during the day when you are not going to be too rushed. If possible, it might be better to go before the market opens or after it closes. A broker is less likely to be interrupted by phone calls while he is talking to you. Simply walk up to the receptionist and ask to speak to a broker. Most firms assign brokers to be broker of the day on a rotating basis. They handle all walk-ins and telephone call-ins on their particular day. If you are going to invest a substantial sum of money, do not be afraid to ask to speak to the manager and have him recommend a broker. This way you are more likely to be directed to someone with experience.

Many people will simply call up and do their business over the phone. I have a number of clients, some with large amounts of money invested, whom I have never met in person. This is the case with most brokers. Usually, these clients have a great deal of investment experience and they like to direct their own investments. But in the beginning, at least, you are better off with a face-to-face interview.

Remember, you are hiring a broker. You are hiring somebody to advise you in how to invest your money. Do not be shy about taking up his or her time with an interview. This does not mean that you are entitled to a broker's undivided attention for half a day. But you do have a right to determine whether he is knowledgeable, whether or not you are going to be able to get along with each other, and whether or not he seems to have your best interests at heart.

A good broker will ask you some questions before he tries to sell you anything. The major rule for any broker is: know your client. If you have not volunteered the information yourself, a broker should determine your financial goals, your tax bracket, and your general financial situation before making an investment suggestion. A married man with three children and making $50,000 a year has different needs from a single individual earning $12,000 a year. Likewise, someone approaching retirement is in a different situation entirely from someone just entering the work force. It is a broker's job to do some probing during the interview. He is not being nosey; a broker has to know something about your financial situation in order to make some intelligent suggestions to you.

So, after visiting a couple of brokerage houses and meeting several brokers, you are ready to make a decision. By the way, you are under no obligation to open an account with a broker just because you sat and chatted for twenty minutes. If you do not feel right for one reason or another, if you feel the broker is not giving you good advice or is more interested in himself than in you, do not be afraid to talk to someone else before deciding.

Many large investors, it should be mentioned, employ an *investment advisor* to direct their investments for them. An investment advisor is in a separate category distinct and apart from a registered representative, or broker. He is a professional advisor who usually works for a percentage of the assets managed for his clients. Some advisors have discretion over their clients' investments, which means they themselves direct the investments through a broker or brokers with whom they work; others merely advise their clients, who may or may not act on the advice on their own initiative. If you have a large portfolio and you do not have the time to spend studying the market and keeping on top of your own investments, you might consider the possibility of hiring an investment advisor.

Opening an Account

Once you have visited a firm and met a broker you would like to work with, the next step is to open an account. When you open an account, you will have to provide your broker with certain basic information. Your broker has to know your full name and address, the kind of account you are opening, your Social Security number or a tax identification number, your citizenship, your home and business telephone numbers, your occupation and place of employment, marital status and name and occupation of your spouse, whether or not you are of legal age, a bank reference, and other pertinent information depending on the kind of account you are opening and the kinds of transactions you are going to make. All this is very basic, and can usually be done in a few minutes following your interview or over the phone the next day. A broker is required by law to obtain as much information as possible. The better your broker gets to know you in the beginning, the better he can service you later on.

In some cases you will be asked for a deposit when you open an account. Normally, this is only for the first transaction. Later you will be able to conduct business over the phone and pay your bills on a settlement date, which, in most cases, is within five business days following a transaction.

As far as the kind of account you should open is concerned, your broker can advise you of the various possibilities. You may want to open a sole proprietorship account in your name alone; a *joint tenants with right of survivorship* account in which case, if one party dies, his ownership interest passes on to the surviving tenant; a *tenants in common* account whereby, upon the death of one tenant, his ownership interest remains in the deceased's estate; a *partnership* account if you are investing with a business partner; or a *corporate account* which is opened in the name of a corporation. Your broker can help you pick one suited to your needs. If you have complex tax considerations, you might want to check with your accountant or tax man to decide the best course of action for you. Some married couples prefer to have individual accounts in each of their names, others prefer a joint-tenant account, others will have both. If you have young children, you may want to open *custodian* accounts for them. This is a good way of investing money for their education while getting a tax break on any income and capital gains. A general rule of thumb is to divide your assets up into several accounts for estate purposes.

Your broker can also set up Keogh and IRA accounts for you if you want separate retirement accounts. The great majority of accounts fall into the categories already mentioned, but in special situations, people open numbered accounts, fiduciary accounts, and others that you will most likely not be concerned about, in the beginning at least.

You can also specify whether you want a *cash* or a *margin* account. In a cash account you pay for everything in full. When you buy on margin, you put up part of the money, say 50 percent, and the brokerage firm lends you the balance and charges you interest on the loan. In the beginning I would advise you to stick to a cash account. Buying on margin can be attractive after you've gotten some experience and feel confident in what you're doing, and you can always switch from cash to margin later on. Most firms have certain minimum equity requirements for margin accounts, and you have to be prepared to meet maintenance calls if the value of your securities declines below a given level. For example, suppose you bought 500 shares of a $20 stock. This transaction would cost you $10,000 plus commission. If you bought on margin and put up $5000, the brokerage firm would lend you the other $5000. Now suppose the stock declines to 10 and your equity is wiped out ($5000 worth of stock minus the $5000 loan equals zero equity). You would have received a maintenance call before this happened to maintain a minimum equity requirement in your account, which means you would have had to come up with additional money to add to your account. Of course, if your stock went up, you would make a greater percentage return on your investment dollars than is possible with a cash account. If this same stock went up to 30, you would double your money; if you had bought it in a cash account you would make only 50 percent.

Just remember that a margin account carries with it an extra element of risk. If you are prepared to accept that, fine. If not, stick to a cash account.

Once you have selected a brokerage house, hired yourself a broker, and opened an account, the fun begins. What are you going to invest in? How do you go about creating a portfolio? To answer these questions, let's talk about strategy.

10

What to Invest In

The first thing to do before investing a nickel is to define your objectives. It makes no sense to start buying stocks, bonds, and other securities before you have analyzed your own individual financial situation and determined what your needs are and what you want your money to do for you. It is not enough to say, "My goal is to make money." Everyone wants to make money, but that means different things to different people. If you are ten years away from retirement, your needs and objectives are not likely to be the same as those of a young widow or divorcee with a moderate income and two small children to raise. If you are in a 25 percent income tax bracket, your situation is not quite the same as someone in a 50 percent bracket. If your fundamentals are taken care of—insurance, home, car, basic necessities—you will have different goals than a young couple planning for marriage with little money to start with.

The classic financial pyramid calls for building a broad foundation first, then looking toward conservative or moderate growth, and finally speculating or risking a small percentage of your assets after your basic and conservative goals have been provided for.

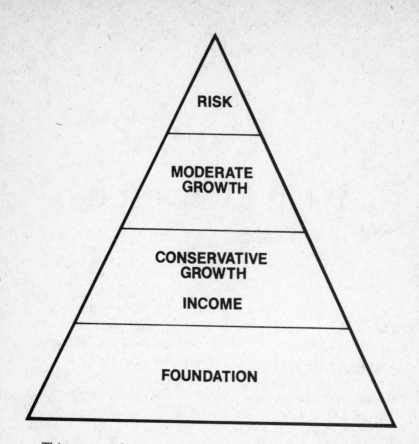

This pyramid is a general guide. Some of us require a broader base than others; some may be willing to put more dollars at risk than you or I. Personal temperament also comes into play. Can you sleep nights if 20 percent of your assets is committed to highly speculative investments? If not, you may be well advised to limit your risk to 5 percent. Someone who can afford it, and who enjoys speculating on the ups and downs of the market, may feel better risking a larger portion of the pyramid.

What all this boils down to is that each individual and each family situation is unique. We can create broad general categories and try to fit people into them. We can say that, under a given set of circumstances, you might be better off doing such and such with your money. Your broker or investment counsellor can point you in a certain direction by making suggestions that seem suitable for your own circumstances. But, in the end, it is you who must make the final decision. After analyzing your own situation, after digesting the advice and suggestions, you must decide on the best course of action.

Now let's look at some possibilities.

Ready Assets

If you have cash that you want to put to work for the short-term, but which you are going to have to use for one reason or another within a few months or a year, your main objective should be safety and liquidity. You want to be sure your principal will be intact when you need it, and you want to be able to get your money back on short notice. Where can you invest it?

If you have $10,000 or more, you can buy treasury bills. T-bills provide you with maximum safety and moderate short-term yield. They also give you a tax exemption at the state and local level. You can buy them with maturities falling on or near the date you are going to need your money. There is a ready market for them, so you can sell them beforehand if you have to.

If you have $100,000 or more, you can buy other money market instruments, such as bankers' acceptances, certificates of deposit, and commercial paper. These are extremely safe and normally give you higher yields than T-bills.

If you have less than $10,000, you can buy into a money market or ready assets fund for as little as $1000. In this case your money is invested in a portfolio of money market instruments, and you can usually get it out on a day's notice. Some of these funds are no-load and some offer checking privileges. So, in effect, you are getting an interest-bearing checking account with this investment. Some investors put their savings in these and utilize them as a combination savings-checking account.

Income

If you are looking for current income to live on or to supplement your ordinary income, you will probably want to invest in securities that offer the highest yields around, consistent with a high degree of safety, of course. These could be debt or equity securities, or a combination of both.

You could invest your money in corporate bonds, the first line of obligation of the issuing corporation. You can buy these in denominations of $1000, and you receive interest twice a year.

Another possibility for you is preferred stocks. Preferred stocks offer high dividends and you can buy as many shares as you can afford. Preferreds are traded on major exchanges and OTC just like common stocks, and the dividends are usually paid quarterly.

You might also want to consider high-yield common stocks as a part of your income portfolio. Utility stocks, particularly, offer high dividends, paid quarterly. In some cases, all or a portion of these dividends may be tax-deferred. At the end of the year, you will receive a statement indicating what portion of the dividend payment is tax-deferred. When you sell the stock, you deduct the amount of tax-deferred income you have received from your original cost and calculate your capital gain, if any. You then pay tax on the capital gain.

For example, suppose you buy a utility stock at 25 and sell it five years later at 30. When you deduct the amount of tax-deferred income you have received during this period from your original investment, the cost of the stock is reduced to, say, 18. Your capital gain is now the difference between 30 and 18, or $12 a share instead of $5 a share.

For minimum amounts of $1000 you can invest in U.S. Treasury notes and bonds and the various government agency securities we discussed. The yields here are not apt to be as high as corporate bond yields, but the degree of safety is considered to be higher.

Another popular investment for people looking for current income is a unit investment trust offering a portfolio of income-producing securities. You can buy into a preferred stock trust or a corporate bond trust in multiples of approximately $1000. You then own a proportionate share of all the securities in the portfolio, and the interest or dividends are paid out in the form of a monthly check. Investors like these because of the monthly payment feature, and because of the diversity they have in a portfolio of different bonds or preferreds.

Another possibility for someone investing for income is a mutual fund. Here you are buying shares in a managed portfolio of income-producing securities rather than in a fixed portfolio.

You will note that the above investments fall generally in the category of long-term investments. You invest long-term to maximize your yield. Liquidity should not be an important consideration when you invest for income. Of course, you can always sell your securities if you have to, but you should understand that your investments are subject to the fluctuations of the market. Your bonds, for example, may be selling below par six months after you buy them. They could be selling above par, but your main concern should be the income they produce over a long period of time.

A final vehicle for the income-oriented investor is writing options on stocks you own. Some investors buy round lots of optionable stocks and then write options on them to bring in additional money on top of the dividends they receive. You can write an option for each 100 shares of stock you own. If you decide on this course of action, you should work with a broker with a solid understanding of the options market. A good broker can tell you which options to write in order to maximize your return. He can also advise you whether to let your stock get called away or to buy back options and rewrite new ones, depending on the situation. An options writing program can produce handsome returns as long as you and your broker understand exactly what is going on.

Tax-free Income

If you are in a fairly high tax bracket, current net income could be an important consideration for you. What constitutes a high tax bracket? Many tax advisors regard about 25 percent as an average break-even point. In other words, if 25 percent or more of your income is going in income tax you should probably begin to think in terms of tax-free income as an important financial objective. Your net income from taxable investments will most likely be lower than the income you can get from tax-free investments. In this regard, your broker can give you general information about tax situations, but you, with the help of your tax advisor, will have a better idea of your position vis-à-vis the IRS than anyone else. If tax-free return is a major concern of yours, what can you invest in?

Municipal bonds and notes are still the most popular form of tax-free investment. You can buy the bonds, in most cases, in multiples of $5000, while the minimum denomination for notes maturing in a year or less is usually $25,000. Most investors buy municipal bonds in bearer form, and the interest is normally paid semiannually.

As in the case of corporate bonds and preferred stocks, you also have the option of buying into unit investment trusts consisting of municipal bonds. These are set up in the same fashion as the others, with multiples of $1000 and monthly interest payments. The major distinction, of course, is that the income here is exempt from federal income tax. Mutual funds have also been established in which your money is invested mostly in tax-free bonds in a managed portfolio, and in many cases you can buy into these for smaller amounts of money.

Tax-deferred income is another important objective for those in the higher tax brackets. Tax-deferred treatment is available in the form of dividends from certain utility stocks. Your broker should have a list of utilities and an estimated tax-deferral provision for the current year. The exact percentage is not determined until the end of the year.

Another possibility for current tax-deferred income is a limited partnership in a real estate investment. Strictly speaking, this is not a tax shelter since we are talking about after-tax dollars. Periodically, some firms market this type of vehicle, which offers relatively high tax-deferred income and a chance for capital growth. You might ask your broker about the availability of these.

Tax shelters, naturally enough, are important to those in the higher brackets. An IRA account if you are an employee, or a Keogh account if you are self-employed, will give you a tax write-off each year. If you are in a 50 percent income tax bracket and want to shelter large amounts of cash, then you may want to ask your broker what kind of shelters he has available for the large investor.

Growth

Perhaps you are not primarily interested in current income of either the taxable or tax-free variety. If you do not mind assuming some risk in order to see your capital grow or appreciate over a period of time, then you might be interested in growth investments. You may have investable cash in the neighborhood of five or ten or fifteen thousand dollars. My own feeling is that people investing upwards of $20,000 should consider putting a major portion, say $15,000, into income and the balance into growth or moderate speculation if they are so inclined. Income becomes especially important when the interest or dividends can begin to change your lifestyle a bit. An extra $1000 or $1500 a year can be significant to middle-income people. With lesser amounts of capital to invest, the income you receive is not all that significant and you might well consider growth for the major part of it. There are no hard and fast rules at work here. Every broker has his own investment philosophy, and my own, for what it's worth, leans more toward the conservative side.

Having decided that growth is your main objective, where do you invest your money? Common stocks are the main vehicle for growth investments. What kind of growth stocks? Again, every broker has his favorite laundry list of stocks to recommend. What I look for first is an industry with good long-term potential. It could be energy or leisure or fast-food or a dozen others, depending on the present economic circumstances. Next, I look for companies within the industries I've selected with a good earnings history and good prospects for the coming year. I then isolate those with reasonable yields and relatively low P/E ratios. (If a company earns $2.50 per share and its stock is selling for $25, the P/E, or price/earnings, ratio is 10). The P/E ratio may be viewed as a barometer of whether the stock is trading at a reasonable price. I also like to check out the high and low for the stock during the current and preceding years. If all the research checks out and I can't find anything to contradict it elsewhere, I then add the stock to my buy list. Don't be afraid to ask your broker to send you a Standard and Poor sheet on a company he recommends so you can read up on it yourself. You might also want to get a copy of the brokerage firm's research report, if any, on the company. When you have worked with a broker for a while and determined that the information you are getting is reliable, you may then decide to follow his recommendations without doing your own homework. It won't take you long to find out how well your broker is doing for you.

Other types of investments for those looking for growth include convertible preferred stocks and convertible bonds. Remember that the yields on convertibles are usually lower than on regular preferreds and bonds since they offer you the possibility of capital appreciation. They tend to track the price movements of the stocks into which they can be converted.

You might also buy discount bonds. Corporate bonds that were issued when interest rates were lower sell for less than the face amount (remember, the rule here is that when interest rates are rising bond prices are falling, and vice versa). Your broker can help you locate good quality bonds selling below par. When the bonds mature you will receive face value for the bonds and realize a capital gain. This investment combines both income and growth features.

Finally, for those among you who would rather not direct your own investments with the help of a broker, you can always buy shares in a growth mutual fund and hope that the professional managers do a better job of it than you might have done.

Speculation

There seems to be a bit of the speculator in most of us. Some of us have the inclination to a greater degree than others. My own philosophy calls for putting a maximum of 10 percent of your investable dollars into a high risk situation. If I had $100,000 to invest, I certainly would not want to put more than $10,000 into a speculative investment. I would probably put $60,000 into tax-free income, $30,000 to $35,000 into conservative growth, and speculate the rest.

What constitutes a speculative investment? There are many volatile stocks listed on the exchanges and traded over the counter that make dramatic price swings. Volatile stocks are considered risky since their price movements can be large and sudden. You have to remember that any stock that advances rapidly in a short period of time can also fall just as quickly. You have to be ready to move in and out of these situations on a short-term basis. These are trading situations. Your major concern is in getting a quick move. It is better to set yourself some parameters beforehand. Some investors will limit their risk to 25 percent on the downside, and they set themselves a profit goal as well. So, if they buy a stock for 20 and it falls to

15, they will sell out to avoid being clobbered. Likewise, if the stock hits their target area for profit, say 25, they will take their profits instead of waiting in hopes of a bigger gain.

A good many people who lose money in stocks do so because they do not sell them fast enough. They may have a paper profit and assume that, since the stock went up a bit, it has to go higher. Next thing, they are looking at a loss. No stock *must* do anything. The market has a life of its own. Sometimes it acts rationally, that is, the way it is expected to behave, but more often than not it will surprise us. It is a reflection of mass psychology, a fickle thing indeed, and difficult to gauge. No one can predict the market with certainty, although some have established better track records than others.

What kind of speculative stocks should you invest in? The method of selection is not all that different from picking quality, long-term growth stocks. The fundamentals—earning history and outlook, capitalization, etc.—should be good. The yields on high-risk stocks are usually very low or nonexistent and the P/E ratios could be considerably higher than they are on better quality stocks. Most brokerage firms publish lists of their stock recommendations broken down by categories: stocks you buy for income, good quality growth stocks, and speculative stocks. Ask your broker for a copy, along with his own suggestions. You might also ask him to send you some recent research reports on different stocks issued by his firm.

If you are going to speculate, you may decide to buy stocks on margin. In a margin account, you pay only a portion of the cost and the firm lends you the balance. If the stock moves the way you want it to, your percentage return will be greater than if you had paid for the stocks in full. The main risk in margin is that you may have to meet maintenance calls if the stocks decline significantly.

Another form of speculation is buying puts and calls. Buying options gives you greater leverage than you get by buying stocks. When you buy options, you have to be willing to risk your entire investment. You are gambling on a stock making a certain strike price (falling to the strike price in the case of *puts*) before a specific date. If it doesn't, you have gambled and lost.

Writing naked options is also a form of speculation. Writing naked options means writing calls on stock you do not own. For example, you might write five Polaroid July 35s for two points each without actually owning the stock. Polaroid is selling at 34. You have brought in $1000 to your account (five options at two points each, or $200 per option). You are fine as long as Polaroid remains below 35. But if it should advance to 38 and is called away from you, you will have to buy it in the market at 38 and deliver it for 35. You will have lost $3 a share, or $1500. You brought in $1000 from the premium, so your net loss is $500. Writing naked options can be done only in a margin acount, and you will have to put up part of the cost of the underlying stock that you are obligated to deliver if it should be called away.

You will also need a margin account if you want to sell short. When you short a stock, you are selling stock you do not own. You do this in anticipation that the stock will go down. Suppose Polaroid is selling at 38 and you feel it will fall to, say, 33. You sell the stock short for the current market price, $38 a share. The brokerage firm lends you the stock, which has to be delivered to the buyer. If the stock falls to 33, you can then buy the stock in the market at the lower price and cover your short position. You pay back the brokerage firm the stock you borrowed, and you make a profit of $5 a share. If the stock goes up instead of down, you may have to start meeting maintenance calls to beef up your declining equity. If the stock stays up, you will eventually have to buy it for more than you sold it to cover your short position. In reality, most investors will buy in enough shares as they need at any given time to meet their maintenance calls.

You can see there are many ways to risk your money if you are inclined to do so. Many people do in the hope of realizing large profits in a short period of time. Just remember, if you decide to speculate, you have to be prepared to accept the losses as well as the gains.

Foundation

If you are still in the process of building your financial foundation, your broker can help you here as well.

One of the more attractive ways of putting money aside for retirement is via a *tax-deferred annuity*. Each state has its own rules and regulations governing annuities, but the basic concept is standard. Since this is an insurance investment, only those brokers who are licensed to sell insurance can help you in this area.

The way it works is this. You put away a lump sum, usually a minimum of $5000. You can add more any time you like, but you are not obligated to do so. Your money earns interest for you, which accrues in your account. This income is *tax-deferred* until such time as you decide to take it out. The idea is, if you leave it there until retirement you will be in a lower tax bracket than you are in while you're working. Your principal is guaranteed against loss and you only pay tax on the income portion as you take it out. When you decide to start taking your money out, you have several ways of annuitizing. You can take it out all at once, have it paid out over your lifetime, have it paid out over a fixed period of time, have it paid out for life with a minimum period guaranteed, etc. The main features of this type of retirement investment are the safety and the tax-deferred treatment of your interest.

An alternative to the annuity concept is to put your money in a municipal bond fund that permits you to reinvest your *interest* back into the fund. In this case, the interest you receive is tax-free rather than tax-deferred. Your principal is not guaranteed since the prices of the bonds fluctuate in the market counter to interest rates. But this is regarded as an extremely safe investment, and if you expect to be in a fairly high tax bracket after retirement, the tax-free status of the income may be enough to offset any other considerations.

IRA and Keogh are considered to be foundation money, since your money is building up in a retirement account.

These are also shelters since they involve pretax dollars, while the above investments must be made with after-tax dollars. IRA and Keogh can be utilized in addition to an annuity or tax-free fund.

Another vehicle for foundation money is a custodian account for your children. By appointing yourself custodian for your children, you can invest money for their education without having the income taxed at your bracket. A suitable investment would be corporate bonds, preferred stocks, or unit investment trusts—sound, high-quality securities offering high income that is taxed at the child's tax-bracket rate.

So far in this chapter, we have talked about the need to analyze your own situation and define your objectives before investing. Once you know what it is you are looking for, you can put your money into income, tax-free or tax-deferred income, growth, speculation, or the creation of your financial foundation. Most people invest with a combination of objectives in mind. Some investors who feel confident in what they are doing prefer to direct their own investments; some follow their brokers' advice exclusively; others follow their own lead with the assistance of their brokers. Pick a system that feels comfortable to you.

What about Commissions?

Many brokers are touchy on the subject of commissions, sometimes with good reason. Lawyers charge fees for their services, and so do doctors. Brokers feel that the commissions they earn are no more than they are entitled to for the professional advice and service they render.

Are commissions too high? Too low? Just right? That depends, to a great extent, on the value you are receiving from your particular broker. Some lawyers are good, and others are terrible. Doctors can save your life or put it in jeopardy. Likewise, some brokers will give you sound advice and put your money to work for you, while others make suggestions which wind up costing you money. If your broker is productive and honest with you, if he takes your interests to heart and regards you as an individual with specific needs and goals, then he is probably worth the money you pay in commissions. If not, if he is incompetent or concerned only about hustling you for sales, then you'd best scout around for someone else.

The commission schedules of most major firms are competitive with one another. If you are dealing with a reputable, established brokerage house, you will be paying more-or-less standardized commissions for any securities you buy. There are firms offering large discounts on various transactions, which, as I mentioned before, can be of value to investors who like to direct their own transactions and do not require the advice and research facilities of a large firm.

Some brokers will negotiate commissions with some of their large trading accounts; others flatly refuse to do so. If you are not investing large sums of money on a regular basis, do not even bother to bring up the subject.

Several of the major firms do offer discounted commissions for smaller investors in self-directed accounts. It is possible to open a special account, sometimes referred to as a share-builder account, if you make your own selections and keep your investments below a maximum figure, usually $5000. Some of these require regular payments, and others allow you to send in money whenever you want to. Normally, you mail in your check indicating the dollar amount of the stock you want to buy. You pick your own stocks and do not deal with a broker.

One way to buy securities without paying any separate commission is to ask your broker to keep you informed of retail offerings: new, or primary, issues of stocks and bonds and public offerings of large blocks of previously issued securities (secondary issues). If your brokerage house is managing or co-managing the offering, or if it is a member of the underwriting syndicate, your broker may be able to take down some of the issue and offer it to you free of commission.

114

You should know that your broker is not doing this as a public service. He is paid so much a share by his own firm for all the stock he sells. His commission is part of his firm's underwriting fee, which is built into the offering price of the securities and, in some cases, it is a larger commission than he would ordinarily earn if he bought the stock for you the regular way in the market. Also, he may be given a quota to fill by his firm, which is committed to selling a given number of shares to the public.

Is this a good or a bad way to buy securities? Anything that goes up after you buy it is a good investment. Some stocks go up after an underwriting, and some go down. There is no way to know for sure beforehand. If it is a quality company and you would like to own its securities anyway, regardless of the underwriting, then it makes sense to buy the securities on an underwriting offering.

Now you know how to go about finding a brokerage firm and a broker, and you know the kinds of things to invest in to suit your particular financial objectives. This is a long way from the bewilderment you may have felt just a short time ago.

In the next chapter we are going to talk about a subject that very few people give any thought to at all: financial planning. In the course of a lifetime, we all build up something called an *estate*. It consists of the sum total of our assets, and most of us are worth a lot more than we realize. Yet, few of us take the time to plan adequately for the future. When you're ready, let's take a look at some basic ideas.

11

Financial Planning

Now that you have lined up a broker and invested some of your money, it is time to give some thought to financial planning. What are you doing to be sure your financial affairs are in order? Have you made the best arrangements for your family and other dependents? What are you doing about the future?

It goes without saying that everyone should have a will. Everyone acknowledges the need for a will, but few of us like to think about it in any great detail. Aside from creating a will, you ought to think in terms of arranging your assets in such a manner that they will most benefit yourself and your family and dependents.

In this regard, we should familiarize ourselves with the basics of a *trust*. Trusts can be valuable protective devices for middle-income people as well as for the wealthy. What is a trust? Simply put, it is a set of written instructions directing that your money and/or other property be handled in a certain fashion. A trust can be incorporated as part of a will. It can be used as a means of reducing your personal taxes, as a source of extra income, as a means of setting up your estate so that your family is benefited the most, or for charitable purposes.

In a moment we'll talk about different kinds of trusts, but

116

first let's discuss the ingredients that go into them. The body of written instructions that spell out how your estate is to be handled is the trust. The person or institution appointed to make sure the instructions are carried out is called the *trustee*. You are the *creator*, the *donor*, or the *settlor*. The instructions regarding the disposal of your assets comprise the *indenture*. The assets are the *corpus*. The *beneficiary* is, of course, the recipient of your assets. When the corpus is disposed of, the trust will have been terminated. If you set this up so that you can call it off any time you want to, you are creating a *revocable trust*. If you do it in such a way that you are giving up your right to change the indenture, you are establishing an *irrevocable trust*. And, if you specify a certain time period for the trust after which the assets return to you, you are creating a *reversionary trust*.

Trusts can be as simple or as sophisticated as you want them to be. They are a means of channeling your property to a person or a number of persons in any manner you see fit. You can channel your money to one person for a period of time, then cut if off and channel it to someone else. You can keep the flow steady and add new beneficiaries at later dates. If you are concerned about someone's ability to handle money properly, you can have a trustee invest it and pay out the income and principal in a prescribed fashion.

By law, a trust cannot last forever. It must have a termination date, but this date need not be during the lifetimes of those mentioned in the trust.

Now that you understand the mystery surrounding trusts, a body of written instructions regarding the disposal of your property, let's talk about the two basic categories they fall into.

Testamentary Trust

There are two kinds of trusts: testamentary and living trusts. We'll take them one at a time.

The first type, the *testamentary trust*, is part of your last will and testament. A will is the traditional method of organizing your affairs. If you fail to make one, you are surrendering to the state you live in your right to dispose of your property. It's as basic as that. Without a will, the state walks in and runs the show. Someone dying without a will is dying *intestate*. The state may or may not dispose of your property the way you would have liked. This is the chance you are taking. No one likes to think about a will because it involves the subject of—let's say it once and get it over with—death. But remember: your property and the well-being of your family are at stake here.

Some people have drawn up their own wills and they have stuck, but you are really better off paying whatever it costs to have a competent lawyer do it for you. You want to be sure the legal requirements for executing and witnessing a will have been complied with. The body of instructions indicating how your property is to be divided after you die is the testamentary trust.

Living Trusts

The second kind of trust, which comparatively few of us think about but, perhaps, more of us ought to, is called a *living trust*. This is a written set of instructions that takes effect while you are still alive.

The main reasons for setting up a living trust have to do with tax advantages. No matter how much you may love Uncle Sam and enjoy paying your taxes, it is good to be aware of the legal means that are available to cut the tax bill.

When you dispose of your property through a testamentary trust, the normal procedure calls for it to be reviewed by a probate court. The court sees to it that everything is legal and the instructions are carried out. Besides being time consuming, probate can be expensive. Lawyers, accountants, appraisers, court costs, and other fees can eat up a substantial portion of the estate.

One of the great advantages of a living trust is that it usually avoids probate court. The trust has already been operating during the life of the donor and it remains in effect after his death. There is no frustrating time lag and no probate expense. Living trusts are also private documents; wills are public. In the case of a large estate, the notoriety of sensational publicity can be avoided with a living trust. (Bing Crosby's financial affairs are known only to his family because he established a living trust, but the details of Howard Hughes' affairs continue to make headlines.) In addition, when you create a living trust you may have a choice of several states to have it written in, which means you can pick the state laws most agreeable to you. A living trust can be written under the laws of the state you live in, the state where the property is located, or the state where a beneficiary or trustee lives. A will, on the other hand, comes under the laws of the donor's home state. Finally, a living trust provides you with the opportunity to make certain changes as your own particular circumstances change. You have control over it while you are alive. You can test it, see how it works, make whatever improvements you think necessary.

Having said all this, we should talk about some of the disadvantages of a living trust that you do not have with a will. First, it is possible you could limit your freedom regarding your property since you have to deal with a trustee who has been appointed to carry out your instructions. You are committed to the terms of the trust. Second, the portion of your property that you keep outside the confines of a living trust will be subject to the normal probate laws. You will need a testamentary trust to dispose of that. Third, a living trust can complicate your tax returns because of the number of records and documents you must keep. Finally, if you have any emotional resistance to apportioning out your property during your lifetime, the tax benefits you achieve may not be worth the intangible costs you have to pay.

119

Remember: Each individual and family situation is unique. Each situation has its own special problems and requirements. Having analyzed all the possibilities, it is up to you to determine the best course of action for yourself.

Now that this caveat has been uttered and taken note of let's look at some different kinds of living trusts.

Do you have children you want to send to college? Do you have an older relative—an ailing parent or grandparent—depending on you for support? If so, you may want to consider the possibility of a *reversionary*, or *short-term*, trust.

A while back I mentioned setting up a custodian account for a child. When you open a custodian account for a minor, you avoid paying income tax at the rate for your bracket, but the assets in the account legally belong to the child (his Social Security number is on the account, and the income is taxed at the rate for his bracket) and pass to the child when he reaches legal age. If you should decide, however, that after paying for your offspring's education you would like the assets to revert to you, a reversionary trust is the vehicle for accomplishing this.

The mechanics are as follows: In most cases, the short-term trust must remain in effect for more than ten years—ten years and one day is fine. (You can arrange it so the property reverts to you upon the beneficiary's death in the event he dies before the trust term is up.) You cannot change your mind during this ten-year period and recall your property without exposing yourself to severe tax penalties. If you let the income from your investment build up in the trust instead of having it paid out, you have what is sometimes referred to as an *accumulation trust*. So, for example, you might buy $10,000 worth of bonds or ten units of a corporate investment trust and leave the principal and interest in the trust to pay off your child's educational expenses. Or, in the case of a dependent relative, you might use the income to cover his living expenses. You will receive a tax break since this money is a gift, and as such it is taxed at a lower rate than your ordinary income. The IRS has special gift valuation tables covering this type of trust. At the end of the ten-year period, the trust is terminated and the assets revert to you.

It goes without saying that any kind of living trust must be drawn up with the help of a lawyer since the laws governing them are fairly complex and they vary from state to state.

A *charitable remainder trust* is irrevocable. Suppose you bought some stocks years ago and they have gone way up in value. If you sold those stocks yourself, you would have to pay a capital gains tax. One way to avoid this tax is to give these securities as a gift to a charity in a fashion that benefits both you and the charity.

You can set up this trust so that the charity sells the stocks (without paying taxes) and *reinvests* the money in a way prescribed by you. Suppose there were $50,000 worth of stocks involved, paying small dividends. If the stock is given to a charity, the $50,000 remains intact, and it can be reinvested in bonds or some other income-producing securities. The income from this new investment will be paid to you during your lifetime and, in addition, you will get a tax deduction for making the gift. Upon your death or at the end of a designated period of income payments to you, the assets in the trust become the property of the charity.

The charity you give your assets to can be an actual charity or any nonprofit institution, such as a church or hospital, that is legally qualified under section 170(c) of the Internal Revenue Code.

One way a charitable remainder trust can be established is as a *unitrust* (with variable income paid out as a percentage of the fluctuating market value of the securities, and not to be confused with "unit investment trusts," which I discussed in chapter five). The variable factor in the unitrust comes into play in this way: Let's say the recipient in a unitrust sells the securities and reinvests the money in a mutual fund. The terms of the trust may call for the donor to receive 7 percent annually (by law, the annual withdrawal must be at least 5

121

percent of the current value of the mutual fund shares). Since these shares will fluctuate in value, the exact dollar figure will vary from year to year.

Another way to establish a charitable remainder trust is as an *annuity* trust (with a fixed dollar amount paid to you). In an annuity trust, the dollar amount paid annually to the donor never changes. In all other respects, an annuity trust is the same as a unitrust. But with an annuity trust you are guaranteeing yourself a fixed income each year; with a unitrust your income may be higher or lower from year to year, depending on the market. In both instances, the charity eventually gets what is left.

This gives you a basic understanding of the concept of trusts. Trusts play an important role in financial planning. There are two basic types: testamentary trusts (wills) and living trusts. All of us should have a will. For some of us, the establishment of a living trust could provide handsome tax advantages. Since living trusts can take so many different forms, they should always be drawn up with the assistance of a lawyer and tax advisor.

Now let's see about some other tax considerations in the buying and selling of securities.

12

Basic Tax
Considerations

The federal tax laws in this country are so complex, and they are currently going through a period of such major "reform," that any attempt to address them in detail is bound to be rendered obsolete within a short time. Still, we can talk about some fundamental tax considerations that are likely to remain in effect for at least a while. The Tax Reform Act of 1976, a document running to over 1000 pages and covering more than 250 separate provisions, is destined to be considerably streamlined during the years ahead. Much of its language is confusing and open to various interpretations. Its impact has been far-reaching. Let's cover some of the basics of this new law and see how they affect our financial transactions.

Capital Gains and Losses

When buying and selling securities, the old rule of thumb has always been: Try to keep your capital gains long-term and your losses short-term. A long-term gain is taxed at half the rate of ordinary income, while a short-term gain is taxed at the full level. Conversely, a short-term loss is fully deductible (up to a maximum of $3000), while you can only take off fifty cents on the dollar for a long-term loss. There has been some talk in Congress and the Carter Administration about changing the tax treatment of gains and losses, but at this writing this system is still in effect.

The Tax Reform Act of 1976 did make substantial changes in the holding period, however. Under the old law, if you held stocks or other capital assets for more than six months before selling them you had a long-term gain or loss; six months or less was considered short-term. As of 1977 you had to hold your securities for more than nine months to qualify for long-term treatment, and on January 1, 1978, this period was increased to more than a year. If you bought stock on January 1, 1978, you have to hold it at least until January 2, 1979, to get a long-term capital gain.

In addition to lengthening the holding period, the new law increased the amount of long-term losses you can deduct each year from your ordinary income. Previously, you were limited to $1000, which meant you needed $2000 in long-term losses to get the full write-off. Any excess had to be carried over to the next year. In 1977 you were permitted to deduct up to $2000 in long-term losses, and in 1978 the maximum increased to $3000. Consequently, if you have $6000 in long-term losses in 1978 you can take off $3000 from your ordinary income. If, heaven forbid, your long-term losses are higher than that, you can carry them forward to the following year. Short-term losses remain fully deductible up to a maximum of $3000 (any excess can be carried over to the next year).

Option Income

For option buyers, all profits and losses on transactions are, by law, short-term gains or losses.

Writers of call options are most dramatically affected by the new law. It used to be that premiums received for writing options were taxed as ordinary income. Today these premiums are computed as short-term capital gains, but since the tax treatment is the same for ordinary income and short-term capital gains, this is significant only in the case of a loss. If you decide you want to hang on to your stock and you buy back the options at a loss, this is now a short-term loss, whereas in the past it was treated as an ordinary loss, and you could deduct the entire amount lost with no upper limit. As of 1978, however, since it is considered a short-term loss, you are limited to a deduction of $3000. Any excess must be carried over to the following year.

Preference Income

Preference income is that percentage of a long-term capital gain that is not taxable as ordinary income. For instance, if you are fortunate enough to have a long-term gain of $5000, 50 percent of it, or $2500, is taxed as ordinary income. The other $2500 is known as preference income. In earlier years, in addition to your regular taxes, you had to pay a tax of 10 percent on all preference income over $30,000. Under the new law, you must pay a 15 percent minimum tax on whatever preference income is left after you deduct either $10,000 or one half of the taxes you owe on other earnings. Confusing? Certainly. The purpose of this change seems to be to make people who somehow avoid paying income taxes pay at least a minimum tax on preference income.

To take an example, suppose that you have a long-term capital gain of $40,000 and a total taxable income of $60,000 (which includes 50 percent of your long-term gain, or $20,000 plus your salary, less deductions and exemptions). Let's assume that your income tax on the $60,000 comes to $22,320. Under the old law you would not have had to pay any tax on the $20,000 preference income (that part of the capital gain not taxed as ordinary income) since the first $30,000 would have been excluded. Under the Tax Reform Act of 1976 you can only deduct either $10,000 or half of your tax liability from the preference income, *whichever is greater*. Since half your taxes comes to $11,160, you can deduct this from the $20,000 preference income and then must pay a tax of 15 percent on the remaining $8,840, an additional $1326.

See how simple it all is? Let's take an aspirin and move ahead.

IRA

The 1976 tax law made some changes for the better in the rules covering IRA. Previously, if you were an employed individual not covered by a pension plan you could shelter up to only $1500 a year. Today you can add an extra $250 a year for an unemployed spouse. Also, you have an extra forty-five days after the end of the tax year to establish an Individual Retirement Account for that year (as has been the case with Keogh plans). This gives you some time after the year is over to see what your tax situation is going to be.

Other Tax Shelters

In years past, you would sometimes have been permitted to deduct from your income more money than you had actually put into a tax shelter. So, for example, an investment of $50,000 in an equipment leasing or film venture might qualify you for a write-off of $100,000 or $150,000. Today, your write-off is limited to the amount you have at risk. Most tax experts agree that real estate and oil and gas shelters were the least hurt by this change, but just about all the others were seriously cut back.

Estates and Gifts

The general thrust of the new tax law is to lower taxes on medium-sized estates by raising the exclusion. The law on gifts, however, is a bit more complicated and will serve to increase gift taxes in most instances.

Previously, when you inherited securities the capital gain was calculated on the fair market value of the gift at the time of the donor's death subtracted from the price at the time you sold them. So, if someone left you stock worth $20,000 at the time he died and you sold it for $28,000 two years later, you had a long-term capital gain of $8000. Today the gain is figured on the price the donor originally paid for the securities or their value as of December 31, 1976, whichever is greater. In most cases, this will probably serve to increase your capital gain and the resulting tax.

Margin Accounts

Under the old system, you were permitted to deduct the interest you paid on money you borrowed in a margin account (remember, when you put down $5000 for $10,000 worth of stock, the firm is lending you the other $5000) up to a maximum of $25,000, *plus* amounts equal to your net investment income, *plus* net long-term capital gains, *plus* 50 percent of any investment interest in excess of these amounts.

The 1976 law limits your deduction against ordinary income to $10,000 plus net investment income. You are allowed, though, to carry any excess over from year to year.

Mutual Funds

Early in 1977, the public was flooded with TV and radio commercials and print advertising from various mutual funds offering tax-free income. This was made possible by the 1976 tax reform law, which allowed mutual funds, for the first time, to invest money in municipal bonds. The stipulation was that the mutuals had to have at least 50 percent of their total assets invested in munis, then they could pass the tax-free income on to their investors. Before this law was passed, if you wanted to buy into a portfolio of municipals, you had to buy shares of a unit investment trust.

Miscellaneous

What we have discussed so far are the major changes made by the Tax Reform Act of 1976 affecting securities and investments. There are other tax considerations you should be aware of.

Bond swaps. This involves selling a corporate bond and using the proceeds to buy another corporate bond. The tax loss at the time of the sale is the difference between the sale price and your cost, or the adjusted book value. To qualify for a corporate bond tax loss swap, the sale must be executed on or before December 31 of the year in which you want the loss, and the bond you buy must differ in some *meaningful* way from the bond you sold. You cannot buy substantially the same bond all over again if you want the IRS to allow the loss. Toward year's end, many of the major brokerage firms publish a list of suggested corporate bond swaps for tax purposes.

Stock dividends. Generally speaking, dividends received in the form of stock instead of cash are not taxable for individual (noncorporate) investors. When you sell stock received as a dividend, your cost is computed using the cost of the original stock you bought, and the holding period is the same as for the original stock. If you have an option to take cash instead of a stock dividend, this rule may not apply. You should always consult with a tax expert on these situations.

Stock Rights. Stock rights are described a bit more fully in part three, "Your Investment Dictionary." For our purposes right now, you should know that if you receive any they are usually tax-free. Stock rights give you the right to purchase more shares of a particular stock at a particular price by a certain date. You can elect to exercise your rights, that is, buy more shares of the stock; you can sell your rights to someone else; or you can let your rights lapse. If you sell your rights you will have a capital gain; if you let them lapse you will be allowed a capital loss; if you exercise your rights, the situation gets a bit more complicated. You *must* allocate the cost basis of the original stock to the new shares bought with the rights if the market value of the rights is 15 percent or more of the market value of the related stock. You *may* make this allocation if this figure is less than 15 percent. You must be sure to keep careful records when stock rights are involved, since, if you sell the stock, you have to know your exact cost basis in order to compute your capital gain or loss. I would strongly recommend consulting a tax expert in a situation such as this. (Your broker should be able to help you by referring questions to his firm's tax department.)

Special corporate deductions. Corporations are allowed a special deduction of 85 percent on dividends received from common and preferred stock. Since preferreds usually have higher yields than common stock, they are a popular investment for corporate investors.

Flat bonds. These offer a potential tax advantage to the speculative investor. Bonds that are in default are sometimes sold at a flat price. You do not have to pay accrued interest when you buy them and, most likely, you can buy them at a deep discount. You are speculating that the corporation which issued the bonds will eventually be able to pay bondholders the back interest plus face value on maturity. If this should happen, you will receive not only face value for the bonds, but all unpaid *interest* as well. In addition, the back interest is not taxable since it qualifies as a *return of capital*. Again, this is strictly a speculative investment.

Mutual funds. These can sometimes offer tax advantages to

the extent that, no matter how short a time you have held the shares, any capital gain dividends you receive are treated as long-term.

Government agency securities. Many of these carry an exemption from state and local income taxes, and you should always ask your broker about this possibility. There are no hard-and-fast rules here, but some agency securities that could offer a local tax exemption include: certain Ginny Mae pass-throughs and bonds of the Tennessee Valley Authority (TVA), banks for cooperatives, federal home loan banks, federal intermediate credit banks, federal land banks, and the U.S. Postal Service. Don't take anything for granted here. Always be sure you ask specifically before buying.

Year-end sales. If you are selling securities to establish a loss for the year, you have until the last business day of the year to make your sale. The trade date itself is the effective date for establishing a loss. If you are selling for a gain, however, *settlement date,* which is five business days following the trade date, is the determining factor. If you want your gain for the present year (because, for example, you expect to be in a higher tax bracket next year), you must time the sale so that settlement date falls on or before the last business day of the year. Your broker can tell you the last day you can sell in order to establish a gain for the year.

If you are thinking of taking a gain or loss for the year, start planning for it ahead of time—certainly before the middle of December. (It may be possible to make a cash sale for a gain if you have waited until the last minute, but there is no guarantee this will be allowed.) Every broker I know is flooded with calls during the last few days of the year from clients who are frantic to get their trades in before the gong goes off. If you call your broker between Christmas and New Year's Day, don't be surprised to be told he is on vacation that week!

Sale-versus-purchase. If you have bought several lots of the same stock at different times, you must identify the particular shares you are selling. So, if you bought 100 shares of RCA in April, 1977, 100 more in June, and 100 more in Feburary, 1978, then decide to sell 100 shares of RCA in, say, June, 1978, you must stipulate which lot of 100 you are selling. If you have possession of the stock, you can deliver the particular shares you want to sell; if your broker is holding them for you in the account, you can instruct him to mark the order ticket "versus purchase," such-and-such a date. This is the way your confirmation will read, so you will have an official record for your taxes. Obviously, the cost of the shares you are selling will determine whether you have a gain or loss, and whether it is long- or short-term.

These tax considerations are by no means all there are but they give you an idea of the kinds of things you should think about when you buy and sell securities. You are not investing in a vacuum. Every financial transaction you make has a tax consequence, and it is good to know the legal means you have available to make these consequences as beneficial as possible. Tax laws are complex and changing all the time, and it pays to keep abreast of new developments.

This brings us to the end of part two. By now you have a better idea than you did when we started of what the various kinds of securities are, how to go about finding a broker, defining your objectives, how to invest in appropriate securities suitable for your needs and objectives, the importance of wills and living trusts in financial planning, and various tax consequences of your investment transactions. Your education so far has been a logical, step-by-step progression toward financial self-confidence. Don't hesitate to review what we have covered so far or to take another look at any particular area you feel you would like to understand more fully.

The next part of the book, "Your Investment Dictionary," has two functions. It will serve as a review, cross-referencing some of the material we have already touched on. And it will serve as a ready-reference dictionary offering definitions, in alphabetical order, of terms with which you are already familiar plus others we have not yet covered.

Part Three:

Your Investment Dictionary

Account Executive

Another name for a stockbroker, registered representative. (See *Registered Representative*.)

Accrued Interest

Interest you have to pay the owner of a bond when you buy it between interest dates. Most bonds pay interest semi-annually. If, for example, a bond pays interest on March 15 and September 15 and you buy this bond on May 15, you owe the previous bondholder two months accrued interest, which will be included in your bill. On September 15, you will receive the entire six months' interest.

Advance-Decline

The number of stocks that went up versus the number of stocks that went down on any trading date. If you ask your broker for the advance-decline during market hours, he can tell you how many stocks are up, how many are down, and how many are unchanged from the previous day's closing prices. These figures are published each day in the financial pages of major newspapers.

Agent

When you buy or sell securities through your broker, and your broker arranges the transaction through a third party, the brokerage house is acting as agent. A broker is a middleman of sorts in all transactions taking place on the exchanges. He is bringing buyers and sellers together, and earning a commission for arranging the trade.

American Depository Receipt (ADR)

When you buy stock in a foreign corporation, most likely you will receive ADRs instead of the actual stock certificates. ADRs are receipts for the actual certificates, which are deposited in a foreign bank. The ADRs are issued by U.S. banks and they guarantee that the certificates will remain on deposit in the foreign bank as long as you own the shares. You are entitled to all benefits and dividends as though you actually held the certificates.

Annuity

An insurance investment that allows you to put away lump sums of money and have the interest accumulate tax-deferred until you take it out. It is usually used to build up a retirement fund. If the interest paid is fixed from year to year, it is a *fixed annuity*; if the interest fluctuates, it is a *variable annuity*.

Appreciation

People investing for growth are looking for capital appreciation. They want to see a sum of money grow into a larger sum, or *appreciate* in value.

Arbitrage

The simultaneous purchase and sale of the same or an equivalent security in order to take advantage of price differentials. For example, if a stock is trading at 30 on the New York exchange and 30¼ on the Pacific exchange, a trader might simultaneously buy it on the New York and sell it on the Pacific to realize an immediate quarter-point profit. The same situation might occur between a convertible stock or bond and the underlying security when they are temporarily out of parity. One who engages in arbitrage is known as an *arbitrageur*.

Ask Price

When you ask for a quote on a stock, bond, or other security, you will get a *bid and ask*. The ask price is the price being asked for stock. Whether or not you can buy it for less depends on the market for the stock: the relative number of sellers and buyers and the prices they are willing to buy and sell for. (See also *Bid Price* and *Quote*.)

Assets

Property owned by an individual, an institution, or an estate. *Net assets* are the property that is left after all debts have been taken into account.

Average Down

To average down is to reduce your cost basis in a security by buying more of it as it falls in price. If you buy 100 shares of RCA at 30 and they fall to 20, you can average down by buying

100 additional shares at 20 and bringing your average for the 200 shares to $25 a share. This way, if the stock moves up again, it only has to make 25 for you to break even.

Baby Bonds

Bonds that are issued with a face value of less than $1000.

Bankers' Acceptances

Bankers' acceptances are money market instruments with maturities ranging up to 270 days. They are irrevocable obligations of banks issued in minimum denominations of $100,000 to facilitate dollar exchanges with foreign banks or to finance transactions in specific commodities. The interest on them is paid in the form of a discount from the face amount when they are bought. BA's are mainly of interest to institutional investors.

Bankruptcy Proceedings

When a corporation's financial situation declines to a point where it can no longer meet its obligation to investors, it may go into Chapter X or Chapter XI under the federal bankruptcy laws. Of the two, Chapter X is the more serious, involving as it does a total readjustment of the company's secured bonds. Chapter XI calls for a reorganization to adjust the unsecured bonds issued by the company.

Bear Market

A market in which stock prices are generally falling. A *bear* is one who expects a further decline in prices. Wall Streeters can and do disagree about how long a decline has to last and how severe it must be before it qualifies as a full-fledged bear market. (See also *Bull Market*.)

Bearer Bonds

Bonds that are not registered in the name(s) of the owner(s). Most municipal bonds are sold in this form. They come with coupons attached, which you clip and present at set intervals to receive interest payments.

Bid Price

Bid and *ask* are the two sides of a price quote on a security. The bid price is the one a buyer is willing to pay. If you are selling it is the price you can get for your securities. (See also *Ask Price* and *Quote*.)

Big Board

Wall Street jargon for the New York Stock Exchange.

Bill

A short-term debt security, maturing in one year or less, as a Treasury bill.

Blue Chips

Stocks issued by substantial, well-established companies enjoying public confidence because of a long history of stability.

Blue chips are considered to be highest-quality investment grade stocks.

Bonds

Long-term debt securities, usually with maturity periods of longer than twenty years. They are issued by corporations, municipalities, states and other levels of local government, the federal government, and various government agencies in order to finance long-term capital requirements. Interest is normally paid twice a year. They are available in many forms, offering a wide bariety of features. (See also *Municipal Bonds*.)

Book Value

The stockholders' equity in the assets of a company after company debts have been paid. When you divide the number of shares of stock outstanding into this equity, you get a figure known as book value per share. Some investors like to compare the price of a stock with its book value to get an idea of whether or not it is a good buy. Most stocks trade above their book value, but just how much above depends on other fundamental factors such as earnings history, earnings projections, yield, capitalization, etc.

Bottoming Out

A term used to describe a stock that has been falling in price but seems to be leveling off and establishing a plateau. The expectation is that the stock will soon begin to rise again. Some investors look to stocks that seem to be bottoming out as good vehicles for investment. (See also *Topping Out*.)

Breakpoint

See *Letter of Intent*.

Broker

A registered representative, account executive. (See *Registered Representative*.)

Bull Market

The opposite of a bear market, a market in which stock prices are generally rising. A *bull* expects prices to advance further. Wall Streeters can disagree over how long or large the rise has to be before it is a genuine bull market. One of the more amusing and insightful definitions of a bull market I've ever heard was offered by Peter Bernstein. He described it as a market where you can buy late and still make money. (See also *Bear Market*.)

Call

The right to purchase 100 shares of a specific stock at a specific price by a specific date. The stock you buy a call on is the underlying stock; the price you can buy the stock for is the strike price; and the date you must buy it by is the expiration date. Calls are now listed on options exchanges, while previously they were traded over the counter. The buyer of calls is speculating that the underlying stock will move up beyond the strike price before the expiration date. If this happens, most buyers will sell the options themselves rather than buy the underlying stock. They are looking for leverage and a quick trading profit. Sellers of calls are known as writers. For the most part, writers are trying to increase their income from stocks they already own. Writing calls is considered a much more conservative investment strategy than buying them. (See also *Option*, *Put*, and *Strike Price*.)

Callable Bonds

Bonds that can be called in by the issuer before maturity. This is usually done if interest rates fall after the bonds are issued and the issuer wants to re-fund its debt. The issuer will call in the old bonds and issue new ones with lower interest rates. To do this, however, it usually must pay the bondholders a call price that is above the face value of the bonds.

Capital Gain

When your investments appreciate, or grow, in value and you sell them, you have a capital gain. A capital gain is long-term if you held the securities for longer than a year, and short-term if you held them a year or less. Your capital gain will be taxed accordingly. If you are taking a loss on your investments, you will have either a long-term or short-term capital loss depending on your holding period. Let's say you buy a stock at 10 and sell it two years later at 15. You have a long-term gain of $5 per share. If you instead sold it at 5 six months after you bought it, you would have a short-term loss of $5 per share.

Cash Account

An account with a brokerage firm in which you pay the full amount for all securities you purchase. (See also *Margin Account*.)

Cash Flow

Cash flow is a measure of a corporation's worth consisting of net income after taxes plus certain intangible charges against income such as depreciation and depletion, which is usually expressed in dollars per share of common stock outstanding.

Certificates of Deposit

CDs are money market instruments issued by commercial banks with maturities ranging from one month up to one year. Minimum denominations are $100,000, so CDs are bought primarily by institutional investors. They are bought at face value and the principal amount plus the interest is paid back at maturity.

Chartist

One who bases his analysis of a particular stock or of the market in general on past performance. Chartists keep graphs or charts showing price fluctuations and make investment decisions based on the patterns formed on the charts. Ordinarily, they are not concerned about fundamental analysis—earnings forecasts and economic outlook—since they maintain that chart formations anticipate the fundamentals surrounding the market. Most major firms offer investment advice based on the findings of both their fundamental and technical analysts (chartists). (See also *Fundamental Analysis, Resistance Level,* and *Technical Analysis.*)

Churning

A practice forbidden by law, though difficult to prove. Some brokers will attempt to generate excessive and unnecessary trading in a client's account in order to make more commissions. They "churn in order to earn." There is sometimes a fine line between heavy speculation and churning, and the amount of activity in any given account can be open to interpretation by the authorities. Generally speaking, an investor who is making money is not going to complain. But a highly active account that is continually losing money should be considered suspect.

Closed-end Fund

A kind of investment company that ordinarily raises money through a one-time public offering of shares. It is organized pretty much the same as any corporation except that its sole objective is to invest shareholders' money in a portfolio of securities. The securities issued by a closed-end company can be listed or traded over the counter, and their market value is determined by supply and demand.

Commercial Paper

Money market instruments issued by well-known corporations with maturities of up to 270 days. They are sold in minimum amounts of $100,000, and the interest is paid in the form of a discount from the face amount when you buy. In effect, commercial paper is promissory notes issued by corporations to meet their short-term financial needs. It is bought primarily by institutional investors.

Commission

In most cases, when you buy and sell securities you will be charged a commission by the brokerage firm handling the transactions. Commissions will vary between firms and according to the size of the transaction, that is, the number of shares traded and the total dollar volume. When you are charged a commission, the brokerage firm is acting as an agent in the transaction.

Common Stock

See *Stock*.

Convertible Securities

Convertible preferred stock can be converted into a set number of common shares. Generally speaking, the price of the preferred tends to track the price movement of the common, so that this kind of preferred offers the investor growth potential as well as income. Convertible bonds can be exchanged for the issuing company's common stock and, occasionally, they may be convertible into preferred stock. The conversion ratio varies from one security to another. When there is no differential between the two prices, they are at parity with each other.

Coupon Rate

The annual rate of interest paid by a bond, expressed as a percentage of face value. If a bond has a 9 percent coupon rate, it pays $90 a year per $1000. This $90 is a fixed return regardless of what happens to the price of the bond. Bearer bonds also carry actual coupons on them. The owner of bearer bonds clips the coupons as they fall due and presents them to receive interest payments.

Cumulative Preferred

A cumulative preferred stock guarantees that any dividends on the preferred that are in arrears must be paid before any common stock dividends are paid. If a corporation misses its dividend payments on cumulative preferred for two quarters, for example, it must pay out the back dividends before resuming payments on its common stock.

Current Ratio

On a company's financial statement, there will be a list of current assets and current liabilities. When you divide the current liabilities into the current assets you get the current ratio.

Current Yield

The rate of interest paid by a bond based on its current market price. If a bond pays 9 percent, or $90, a year per $1000 face value, and the price of the bond falls to $900, the current yield is 10 percent ($90 divided by $900 equals 0.10, or 10 percent). The current yield is always fluctuating with the price of the bond, whereas the coupon, or nominal, yield remains the same. (See also *Yield*.)

Custodian Account

An account opened by an adult in custody for a child. The assets in the account legally belong to the child, and he comes into full ownership of them upon reaching legal age. Some parents open custodian accounts for their children to set aside money earmarked for educational expenses. The income from the investments is taxed at the rate for the child's tax bracket, thus providing tax benefits for the parents.

Day Order

A day order is good only for the day you give the order. If you tell your broker to buy 100 shares of ASA at 22, day only, your order is good for that day's trading. If your broker cannot buy ASA at 22 (perhaps it has been trading at 22¼ and higher all day), the order will be canceled when the market closes. (See also *Good 'til Canceled* and *Limit Order*.)

Debenture

An unsecured corporate bond, that is, a bond backed only by the reputation and financial record of the issuing corporation. It represents an unconditional promise by the corporation to pay the annual interest and the principal on the date of maturity. A debenture is not backed by any kind of physical assets. (See also *Secured Bond*.)

Debt Securities

Bonds, notes, bills, and other debt obligations of the issuing entity. When you buy a corporate bond, for example, you are lending the company money. Municipalities borrow money by issuing municipal bonds.

Defensive Stocks

Stocks that give you the best protection against major drops in the market. Ordinarily, they do not make major swings in either a bear or a bull market. People who buy defensive stocks are looking to preserve their capital and stay ahead of inflation. Consequently, they look for stable stocks with high yields, such as utilities.

Dilution

What happens when convertible securities are converted into the common stock of the corporation. The number of shares of outstanding common stock is increased and earnings have to be spread out, resulting in a lower earnings-per-share figure. Hence, there is a thinning out, a dilution.

Discount

When the price of a bond falls below face value, it is said to be at a discount. A $1000 bond trading at $980 is at a slight discount. This same bond trading at $500 is at a deep discount. The interest on certain money market instruments is paid in the form of a discount from face value when you buy them.

The term is also used as a verb: discounting the news. Some stocks will rise or fall in anticipation of good or bad news. When bad news is expected a stock will sometimes make its decline beforehand; when the news actually breaks, it is not unusual to see the price stabilize or even go up a bit. The news had already been discounted, and the stock dropped in value before the news came out. The reverse is true on good news (which is one reason why it is sometimes too late to buy a stock when you read good news on it in the newspapers).

Discretion

When you give someone power of attorney over your account, you are giving that party discretion. He has the right to make transactions in your name. Several major brokerage firms will not permit their brokers to take discretion over a client's account for several reasons, the main one being that it is difficult to withstand charges of conflict of interest if a dispute should arise with the client. The temptation for a broker is to trade an account too much, churn, since this generates commissions. When this type of arrangement is permitted by a firm, it is referred to as a discretionary account.

Diversification

To diversify is to spread your investment dollars among various investment situations. The investments could be spread among different industry groups, different stocks within the same industry, or stocks in companies in different parts of the country and in different foreign countries to participate in local economic activity. Diversification can also take the form of having a mixed portfolio of bonds, preferreds, and common stock; or a diversified bond portfolio of debt securities with different maturities. A combination of these ingredients would also be considered diversification. The idea is to achieve balance by spreading out the risk.

Dividend

Cash or stock that is distributed to shareholders, representing their proportionate share of the profits. Cash dividends on both preferred and common stock are usually paid out quarterly.

Dollar-Cost Averaging

A system whereby an investor will buy a fixed-dollar amount of a stock at regular intervals, rather than buy a set number of shares. For example, instead of buying 50 or 100 shares of stock at random, you put, say, $50 or $100 a month into the stock. When the stock is low you will be buying more shares for the same amount of money than you will be when the stock is trading at a higher price. Your *average* cost per share will be lower than the average market price per share during a given period because you are buying more shares at lower prices than you are when the stock is high. This is a simple method of establishing a position on a stock at the lowest average cost to you over a period of time. Some brokerage firms allow you to do this in a sharebuilder account, which also offers a reduced commission schedule.

Dollar-cost averaging also works when you buy other commodities. It is better to buy gasoline, for instance, by the dollar amount rather than by the gallon, assuming that you buy it in different stations. If you ask for $5 or $10 worth of gas instead of ten gallons or a tankful, you will be buying more gasoline for your money when the price is lower and fewer gallons when the price is higher. Over a period of time your average cost will be lower since you took advantage of the lower prices.

Dow Jones Averages

Indexes of the average prices of stocks divided into three groups: industrials, transportation, and utilities. The figures are quoted in the financial pages of major newspapers each day. The most important among them is the industrial average, which is a statistical average of thirty major industrial stocks. The DJIA is considered a key indicator of the relative health of the market.

Downtick

A drop in the price of a stock from its previous price. For instance, when a stock slips from 34¾ to 34½, it is downticking. (See also *Uptick*.)

Earnings per Share

When you take a company's earnings and divide it by the number of common shares outstanding, you get the earnings per share. This is an important figure for investors who are looking for stocks they consider to be undervalued in price. (See also *Price/Earnings Ratio*.)

Equities

Equities represent shares of ownership in a corporation. The two kinds of equities are preferred and common stock.

Estate

The sum total of your assets and liabilities. When you die, that part of it not placed under the terms of a living trust beforehand will be subject to the probate laws. (See also *Living Trust* and *Trust*.)

Ex-dividend Date

Cash dividends on stocks are ordinarily paid quarterly. If you buy a stock before the ex-dividend date, you will be entitled to the dividend for that quarter. If you buy it when it *goes ex*, you are buying it ex-dividend, or without the dividend for that quarter. You have to wait until the next quarter to start collecting dividends.

Execution

When you give an order to a broker, you are hoping for an execution. This means the order you gave him has been fulfilled. The broker will call you back to tell you you got an execution. If it was an order to buy, he may say, "Your order was *filled* at 35,"—or whatever price he bought it for. If it was a *sell* order, he could say, "We *got it off* at 35." In either case, you have yourself an execution.

Face Amount

The principal amount on a debt security. The amount of money you will get back when the security matures.

Fixed Income

Income from an investment that remains the same for the life of the investment. The interest on bonds and dividends from preferred stocks are fixed. You can also opt for a fixed income under an annuity contract. Dividends from common stock, on the other hand, may fluctuate.

Floor Broker

A broker who executes an order for an account executive on the floor of an exchange. Suppose you call your broker and tell him to buy 100 shares of RCA, which is traded on the New York Stock Exchange. Your broker will call or wire (depending on the firm he works for) your order to the floor of the NYSE, and a floor broker will go to the specialist's booth that trades in RCA and buy the stock. The major firms employ their own floor brokers, while some of the smaller firms use floor brokers of other firms to execute their orders for them.

Fractional Shares

When you buy stock by the dollar amount, you will get exactly the number of shares to the fraction that your dollars will cover. The same may be true when you buy shares in a mutual fund. The partial shares are called fractional shares. Occasionally, when a stock splits there are fractional shares involved.

Fundamental Analysis

The system of projecting trends in a company, an industry, or the market in general by analyzing the financial and economic details. Fundamental analysts make investment suggestions based on a broad spectrum of financial data. (See also *Chartist* and *Technical Analysis*.)

Glamor Stocks

Stocks that seem to have caught the public's eye for one reason or another. At any given moment, there will be a company, a group of companies, or an industry that suddenly receives a lot of publicity in print or through word-of-mouth. There will be a flurry of activity in these stocks as investors start buying into them, driving the prices up. Often there is no apparent reason why a stock is going up other than the fact that it is going up. Heavy buying generates more heavy buying, and no one wants to miss the boat. The trick here is to get out of these stocks before everyone else does and start buying new glamors.

Going Public

A privately held company is one whose stock is owned by a few people, sometimes a family, and not traded on the market. When a private company decides to make a public offering of its stock to whomever wants to buy it, it is going public.

Good 'til Canceled (GTC)

An order that remains open for thirty days; also called *open order*. If RCA is trading at 29 and you tell your broker to buy it at 28 and leave the order open, your order will stay in effect for thirty days. If, at any time during this period, the stock falls to 28 or lower, your order will be filled. GTC orders are usually initiated by people who either want to buy a stock at a certain price *but no higher*, or sell at a certain price but no lower. (See also *Day Order, Limit Order,* and *Open Order.*)

Growth

An investment objective of an investor looking for appreciation of his investment dollars over a period of time. Growth is ordinarily a long-term objective. Investing for quick profits is referred to as trading, or speculating. Investing in a stock because of the dividends it offers without regard for its growth potential is known as investing for income.

Hedging

A means of protecting oneself against loss with counterbalancing investments. There are commodities hedges, which involve buying a futures contract on a commodity you are already pledged to deliver by a certain date. And there are securities and options hedges, which call for being long and short the same item simultaneously. To hedge is to minimize the risk of an investment. For example, if you bought a stock at 50 you might simultaneously buy a put at 50 on it so that you could sell the stock for 50 if it should fall below that price during the life of the option. It amounts to an insurance policy to protect the investor against an adverse price movement.

Hot Issue

Theoretically, a hot issue is one that goes up in value immediately after it is offered to the public. The trouble with hot issues is that they are easier to recognize after rather than before the event.

Hypo(thecation)

If you decide to open a margin account, you will be asked to sign a hypo, or hypothecation, agreement. This means that you are pledging your securities as collateral when you borrow money to buy securities. If the stocks you buy on margin decline substantially and you are unable to meet your financial commitment, the brokerage firm is authorized to sell your securities to pay off the debt. (See also *Maintenance Call* and *Margin Account*.)

Income

When you invest for income you are looking for a high current return on your investment dollars consistent with a high degree of safety of principal. Bonds, preferred stocks, and high-yielding good-quality common stocks are prime vehicles for an income portfolio.

Indexing

An investment strategy involving the creation of a portfolio tailored as closely as possible to the Standard and Poor 500 stocks. The idea is that the S&P 500 have a relatively good performance record and that you are sometimes better off with an index portfolio than you are trying to beat the averages.

Indicators

Periodically, the government publishes a list of indicators designed to tell us how the economy is doing. These are broken down into three categories: leading, coincident, and lagging indicators. *Leading indicators* usually give us a preview of what to expect on the economic front several months in advance. These include stock prices, corporate profits, new unemployment claims, consumer installment debt, and other factors. *Coincident indicators*, which include the Index of Industrial Production, long-term bond yields, and retail sales, fluctuate simultaneously with movements in the business cycle. *Lagging indicators* pretty much confirm what has already happened and, for this reason, are sometimes called confirming indicators. Obviously, from the investor's point of view, the leading indicators are of the greatest importance.

Insider

Officers or directors of corporations. Their transactions in their own companies' securities are closely regulated by the Securities and Exchange Commission (SEC). Inside information is that which is known by insiders but not by the general public. Brokers are prohibited from executing orders if they know that their clients are acting on inside information.

Interest

Interest, as it pertains to the securities business, is the income you receive from bonds and other debt securities. It is the annual cost the issuer must pay in order to borrow money.

Investment Advisor

A professional financial advisor who usually works for a percentage of the assets managed. He is not a broker and is not licensed to trade securities. (See also *Registered Representative*.)

Investment Banker

When a corporation or other institution needs to raise money by offering securities for sale to the public, it will usually call upon the services of an investment banking firm. If, for example, a company wants to float a new issue of common stock, investment bankers form a syndicate to help market the stock to the public. The terms of these agreements can vary from one offering to the next.

Investment Club

An organization formed to pool the investment dollars of its members in order to invest in a securities portfolio. The idea is for small investors to come together and participate in a more diversified portfolio than they could establish on their own.

Investment Objectives

The goals you hope to achieve when you invest your money. Broadly speaking, you can invest for income, tax-free income, tax-deferred income toward retirement, tax shelters, growth, speculation, or any combination of the above. It is important to understand your own situation and formulate your objectives before you invest.

Joint Account

There are two types of joint accounts. The more common for married couples is *Joint Tenants with Rights of Survivorship* (JT/WROS), in which, upon the death of one party, all the assets in the account automatically pass on to the survivor. The other is *Joint Tenants in Common*, in which half the assets remain in the estate of the deceased. This is more common with business partners. Some tax advisors recommend that married couples have sole proprietorship, or individual, accounts instead of JT/WROS. It might be worthwhile checking with your accountant or tax advisor to determine the best type of account for you.

Keogh and IRA

Tax-sheltered retirement plans. Keogh is for self-employed people who want to put away up to 15 percent (current maximum is $7500 per year) of their income for retirement purposes. IRA is for employees not already covered by a retirement plan. The current IRA maximum is $1500 per year plus $250 for an unemployed spouse.

Letter of Intent

When you buy into a mutual fund, there ordinarily are breakpoints, or dollar levels, at which the sales charge diminishes. For example, an investment of $25,000 might carry a smaller charge than investments below this figure. A letter of intent in which you agree to invest the breakpoint figure or more in a period not to exceed thirteen months entitles you to the lower sales charge. The salesperson must inform you of all break-point levels beforehand.

Leverage

A speculative device that enables investors to make large profits with relatively small amounts of money. Buying options provides one form of leverage. To obtain leverage, you usually have to be prepared to risk your entire investment.

Limited Partnership

A type of arrangement used in many tax shelters. It provides you with a means of investing in a business and using the deductions in the early years to offset regular income. Your legal liability is limited to what you have invested, hence the name.

Limit Order

An order to buy at a certain price but no higher, or to sell at a certain price but no lower. When you put a limit on an order, you can make it for the day only or good 'til canceled. (See also *Day Order* and *Good 'til Canceled*.)

Liquidity

Liquidity means that you can get your cash back out of your investments on short notice. Securities that permit you to do this are *liquid* investments.

Listed

When stocks or bonds are traded on one of the major exchanges, they are said to be listed securities. Securities that are not listed are traded over the counter (OTC). The securities exchanges have minimum financial requirements for a company to qualify for listing, but many corporations that could meet these requirements choose to remain unlisted for various reasons. (See also *Over the Counter*.)

Living Trust

A set of instructions governing your estate (or part of it) that goes into effect while you are alive, as distinct from a testamentary trust, or will, which goes into effect after death. There are different kinds of living trusts, and they must be created with the help of a lawyer. They are usually created to avoid probate and to take advantage of a lower tax schedule. (See also *Estate* and *Trust*.)

Load

Another name for a sales charge. (See *No-load*.)

Long

When you buy a security, you are long the security. If you leave it with the brokerage firm instead of taking actual possession of it, it is long in your account (See also *Short*.)

Long-term

To establish a long-term capital gain for more beneficial tax treatment, you must hold on to it for longer than a year. Long-term capital gains are taxed at half the rate of short-term capital gains.

Long-term has a different meaning when it applies to debt securities. A bond is a long-term obligation, which means it has a maturity period of more than twenty years. (See *Short-term*.)

Maintenance Call

When you buy stocks or other securities on margin, you could be subject to a maintenance call if the market value of your securities falls below a certain level. This means you will have to send in additional cash or securities to keep the equity in your account above a prescribed level. These requirements change from time to time according to the mandates of the SEC. (See also *Hypo*[*thecation*] and *Margin Account*.)

Margin Account

An account that permits you to buy securities without putting up the full amount for them. So, for example, if you buy $20,000 worth of stocks you may have to put up only $10,000 and the brokerage firm will lend you the other $10,000. If you do this you are looking for leverage. If the stocks go up, you will make a greater percentage return on your investment than had you paid for them in full. If the stocks go down substantially, however, be prepared to answer a maintenance call. (See also *Cash Account* and *Maintenance Call*.)

Market Order

When you give your broker an order to buy or sell a stock at the best available price, you are giving him a market order. A market order is the only kind that is guaranteed an execution the same day. You are buying or selling at the market.

Maturity

The date upon which your debt securities mature, that is, the date when the issuer must pay back the face amount of the securities. If you buy $10,000 worth of twenty-five-year bonds and collect interest on them for twenty-five years, you will get your $10,000 back at maturity. You could sell them beforehand, of course, for their market value at the time.

Money Market

The financial market established to supply short-term cash needs. The government, banks, corporations, and other institutions issue debt securities called money market instruments, which mature in a year or less, in order to raise money for their short-term requirements. The major money market instruments are Treasury bills, bankers' acceptances, certificates of deposit, and commerial paper. (See also *Bankers' Acceptances, Certificates of Deposit,* and *Commercial Paper.*)

Municipal Bonds

Munis, as they are sometimes called, are long-term debt securities issued by municipalities, villages, counties, states, and various municipal authorities. The interest on them is exempt from federal income tax and, in some instances, from state and local income taxes as well. (See also *Bonds*.)

Mutual Fund

A mutual fund is an open-end investment company whose main function is the investment and management of investors' money. It is an open-end company since additional shares are continually offered to the public after the initial offering. Mutual funds can be invested for growth, income, tax-free income, or a combination of objectives.

No-load

A no-load fund is a mutual fund that does not charge the investor a sales fee. *Load* is just another name for a sales charge. Paying a front-end load means that you are paying most of the sales charges in the early years of your investment.

Note

A note is a medium-term debt security, ordinarily maturing in anywhere from one to ten years.

Odd Lot

Shares of stock bought and sold in amounts less than 100 shares. Traditionally, odd lot investors were charged a differential of about one-quarter of a point (25 cents; one point is a dollar) for odd lot investments. In recent years, however, several major firms have begun executing odd lot transactions without the differential. If you intend to do odd lot business, check into this before selecting a brokerage firm. (See also *Round Lot.*)

Odd Lot Theory

A rather cynical theory that holds that the small investor is always wrong—if you want to know whether to buy or sell, wait and see what the odd lotters are doing, then do the opposite. Like most theories, it works sometimes and sometimes not. The size of your investment is no guarantee of success—or failure.

Open Order

The same thing as a good 'til canceled order. It remains in effect for thirty days, when if it has not been executed, it will automatically be canceled. (See also *Day Order*, *Good 'til Canceled*, and *Limit Order.*)

Option

The right to buy or sell 100 shares of a particular stock at a particular price by a particular date. (See also *Put* and *Call.*)

Over the Counter (OTC)

A negotiated market where stocks, bonds, and other securities that are not listed on the securities exchanges are traded. Most of these transactions are made over the telephone among various brokers whose firms make a market in the securities. Currently, there is a move underway to evolve toward a central electronic marketplace for all transactions, which means that all securities trading will take on more and more of the aspects of the OTC market. (See also *Listed*.)

Painting the Tape

An illegal practice whereby various individuals acting in consort will enter matched orders through different brokers in order to create the illusion of heavy trading in a particular stock. When buy and sell orders for the same stock are entered at the same price and there is no change in beneficial ownership involved (that is, the trades are canceling one another out so that there are no profits involved), these transactions may be viewed as an attempt to paint the tape and manipulate the market. (See also *Wash Sale*.)

Paper Gains and Losses

A paper gain is an appreciation in the price of a stock that is not sold to realize a profit. For example, you buy a stock at, say, 25 and watch it go to 30, but you decide to hang on to it instead of selling it to convert your paper gain into a dollar profit. A paper loss is just the opposite.

Par

Par value on common stock is the dollar value assigned to it when it is issued. This figure is primarily for bookkeeping purposes and has little if any relationship to the market value of the stock. In the case of preferred stock, par value is important when it is the amount upon which the investor's dividend is calculated—8 percent of $100 par value, for instance. The par value of a bond is the face amount, or the amount the issuer must pay back to you when the bond reaches maturity.

Penny Stocks

Wall Street jargon for stocks that are selling at very low prices. Most major firms regard anything selling for less than $3 as a penny stock. A penny stock is not necessarily a low-quality investment, but in most cases, it is speculative and calls for some caution before plunging in.

Pink Sheets

The great majority of stocks are traded over the counter and, for this reason, there is not enough room to publish them in the OTC columns of the newspapers. To get price quotes on most of these issues, your broker must consult the pink sheets available in his office. The pink sheets list the names of the stocks, trading symbols, if any, recent bid and ask prices, and the names of the brokerage firms making a market in them.

Portfolio

The total of all your investments. Most small investors regard a portfolio as something for the rich, yet most of us have some sort of a portfolio. Cash, itself, is an investment. So is your house, your insurance policies, and any securities you own. You should balance your portfolio so that your investments are working for you in the best possible way.

Premium

When a bond is trading above par, above its face value, it is said to be trading at a premium. The term *premium* is also used in the options market. When you write or sell calls on stocks you own, the money you receive is your premium.

Price/Earnings Ratio

Ratio of the price at which a stock is trading to its earnings per share. If, for example, a company is earning $2.50 per share and it is trading at 25, it is trading at 10 times earnings, and its P/E ratio is 10. (See also *Earnings per Share.*)

Primary Market

If a company decides to offer a new issue of stocks or bonds to the public in order to raise capital, the usual procedure is to arrange with investment bankers to form an underwriting syndicate to help market the securities. This initial offering of new securities is referred to as the primary market. (See also *Secondary Market.*)

Principal

The amount of money committed to an investment. If you invest $10,000 in bonds at 8.5 percent interest, the $10,000 is your principal and the $850 a year you will receive from this investment is your income.

Prospectus

When a new issue of securities is to be offered to the public, the SEC requires that a prospectus be sent to potential buyers. The prospectus is a formal statement regarding all the facts and figures pertaining to the securities involved.

Put

The right to sell 100 shares of a specific stock at a specific price by a specific date. Puts and calls are both listed on options exchanges. The buyer of a put is speculating that the underlying stock will fall below the strike price before the expiration date. If this should happen, the put will rise in value and the investor will be able to sell it for a profit. Sellers, or writers, of puts are hoping that the underlying stock will not decline in price, in which case they will have received a premium for the puts and they will not have to buy the underlying stock at a price above its market value. (See also *Call*, *Options*, and *Strike Price*.)

Quote

When you ask your broker for a quote on your stocks or bonds, you are really asking for three prices. By punching out some numbers on a machine, your broker can tell you the current market price as well as the bid and ask prices. (See also *Bid Price* and *Ask Price*.)

Random Walk Theory

The random walk theory holds that, since stock prices are basically unpredictable, you can do as well buying stocks at random (taking a random walk) as you can by basing your decisions on technical and fundamental analysis. The random walkers maintain that the market behaves irrationally more often than not, and it is therefore fruitless to try to impose a rationale on it.

Rating

Bonds, preferred stocks, and some other securities are rated for quality by rating services, the main ones being Standard and Poor, Moody, and Fitch. The securities are assigned a letter rating, ranging from triple A down through C and, in some cases, even D.

Redeem

When your bonds and other debt securities reach maturity, they are up for redemption, which means the issuer has to redeem them by paying you back the face value. Sometimes issuers will redeem bonds before maturity, as in the case of callable bonds.

Regional Exchange

The New York and American Stock exchanges, which are presently planning a merger, are the two national exchanges. Others, such as the Boston, Midwest, and Pacific exchanges, are called regional exchanges.

Registered Representative

Stockbroker, account executive. The SEC requires that registered reps be licensed in the various states their clients live in.

Sometimes they must pass a licensing examination, while some states will honor licenses granted by certain other states.

Registered Securities

Corporations that want their securities listed for trading on the major exchanges must file for registration with the SEC. When the SEC registers a stock, it is not passing judgment as to the quality of that stock as an investment vehicle, but merely ascertaining that the company has met the minimum financial requirements for listing. OTC stocks and those traded only on certain small exchanges with low volume do not have to be registered. Many excellent companies choose not to be listed in order to avoid the paperwork involved in filing for registration. (See also *Listed*.)

Resistance Level

A resistance level for a stock is a price at which, for one reason or another, heavy selling, or profit-taking, occurs, which makes it difficult for the stock to advance to a higher price level. For instance, a stock may advance strongly from 22 to 28. All of a sudden, heavy selling will take place in the stock, driving the price down to 24. The stock begins a new advance, approaching 28, when again heavy selling sets in, dropping the stock down. For some reason it is difficult for the stock to advance beyond 28. This price is now established as a resistance level. Many investors like to go in for quick profits, trying to catch a stock on the way up and then selling it when it nears a resistance level. Chartists like to keep graphs of these price movements and observe if stocks can break through previous resistance levels. When this happens, many chartists view it as a sign that the stock will keep advancing to new highs, that is, keep moving up until it encounters a new resistance level. (See also *Support Level* and *Chartist*.)

Rights

When you buy common stock, you usually have the right to maintain your proportionate share of ownership in the corporation. If the company decides to come out with a new issue of common stock, thereby increasing the total number of shares outstanding, you will receive a number of stock rights allowing you to buy a certain number of the new shares at a certain price by a certain date. You then will have the choice of exercising your rights (buying the stock), selling your rights, or letting them expire (lapse worthless).

Risk

The element of uncertainty in any investment you make. There are virtually riskless investments, such as Treasury bills, which are guaranteed by the federal government; low-risk investments, such as bonds and good-quality preferreds; and medium- and high-risk investments. Generally speaking, you should only take high risk with a relatively small proportion of your investment dollars.

Round Lot

A stock transaction executed in multiples of 100 shares. One hundred, 300, 700, and 1000 are all round lots. One hundred and fifty shares is a round lot and an odd lot. (See also *Odd Lot*.)

Rule of 72

A simple formula for determining how long it will take you to double your money at a fixed rate of interest that is reinvested and compounded. You just divide the number 72 by the rate of interest you are getting, and the answer is approximately the number of years it takes to double your money. So, for example, if you have an annuity paying 7.2 percent a year with the interest reinvested and compounded, it will take you ten years to double your money (72 divided by 7.2 equals 10).

Secondary Market

Trading in *new* issues of securities offered to the public is the primary market. Subsequent trading in these securities is done in the secondary, or after, market. The secondary market provides liquidity. (See also *Liquidity* and *Primary Market*.)

Secured Bond

Corporate bonds that are backed by various assets of the issuing corporation are said to be secured. The securing assets can be real estate, equipment, securities in independent companies or subsidiaries of the issuing corporation, etc. (See also *Debenture* and *Unsecured Bond*.)

Securities and Exchange Commission

In 1934 the U.S. Congress passed the Securities Exchange Act, which established the SEC as the watchdog agency regulating securities transactions. The SEC was empowered to make rules and regulations governing various aspects of the securities business and to take disciplinary measures in the event of violations. Actually, the various securities exchanges and the National Association of Securities Dealers do most of the police work under the supervision of the SEC.

Security

Securities are divided into two broad categories: debt and equity securities. Debt securities include bonds, notes, bills, and various debt obligations issued by different institutions. Debt securities represent money borrowed by the issuer. Equities such as common and preferred stock represent shares of ownership in the issuing institution.

Selling Short

Selling stock you do not own. You sell at a certain price in anticipation that the stock will go down afterward. The brokerage firm lends you the stock, which is delivered to the purchaser. Later on, you hope to buy the stock at a lower price in order to cover your short position, that is, pay back the borrowed stock to the brokerage firm. Short selling is regarded as a speculative investment strategy.

Selling Short Against the Box

A short sale against the box is done almost exclusively for tax purposes. Suppose you have a capital gain in a stock that you would like to take, but you do not want to pay a capital gains tax for the current year. For tax purposes, it may be more advantageous for you to postpone the capital gain until the following year. You can lock in your profit by selling short against the box, selling the stock short and hanging on to your own shares. After the first of the year you can then deliver your own shares to cover your short position, and your tax liability will then be for the year in which you delivered your own stock. You succeed in locking in your capital gain and postponing your tax liability until the following year with this maneuver. This type of tax hedge should be undertaken only with expert tax advice. (See also *Short.*)

Settlement Date

The date by which you must pay for securities you buy or deliver securities you sell. In most cases, it falls on the fifth business day following the execution of an order.

Shareholders

The owners of a corporation. They are owners of stock and, therefore, equity in a company.

Shares

Units or certificates of ownership in a corporation. It is the denomination in which stock is bought and sold.

Short

The opposite of a long position. When you sell stock without owning it, you are short the stock. When you sell options you are short the options. (See also *Long, Selling Short,* and *Selling Short Against the Box.*)

Short Interest

Periodically, the major exchanges will report the short interest figures currently outstanding. These are the number of shares of various stocks that are short as a result of short selling and, to a lesser extent, of arbitrage dealings. Some investors like to examine these figures for an indication of bullishness or bearishness among speculative investors. (See also *Arbitrage, Bear Market,* and *Bull Market.*)

Short-term

When you sell securities after holding them for a year or less, you will have a short-term gain or loss. The general rule is to try to keep your gains long-term (taxed at half the rate) and losses short-term (fully deductible).

In the case of debt securities, *short-term* usually refers to maturity periods of a year or less, as in the money market. (See also *Long-term.*)

Sinking Fund

Money set aside in a special fund by a corporation or municipality to meet obligations on various bonds and, in some instances, preferred stocks.

Specialist

A member of a stock exchange whose job it is to maintain a fair and orderly market in the securities assigned to him. On the floors of the exchanges there are specialists' posts where transactions in particular securities are executed. Recently, there has been a move to change the role of the specialists by making them more competitive. The evolution toward a central electronic marketplace is also apt to have a significant impact on their operations.

Speculation

Speculation is the type of investment strategy that calls for the assumption of a relatively high degree of risk in order to realize substantial profits. Speculators are ordinarily more interested in short-term trading.

Spread

The word *spread* can mean different things in different situations. In the case of a stock or bond quote, the spread is the difference between the bid and ask prices. In arbitrage dealings, it is the differential in the price of the same (or substantially the same) security on different exchanges. With convertible securities, a spread occurs when the convertible and underlying securities are out of parity. This is also an arbitrage situation. And a spread can also be an options strategy, as in the case of bull, bear, and butterfly spreads. (See also *Ask Price, Bid Price, Convertible Securities, Option,* and *Underlying Stock.*)

Stock

Stocks are equity securities representing shares of ownership in the corporations which issue them. Stocks are divided into two broad categories: common and preferred. *Common stock* ownership carries with it the right to vote and various other rights, while preferred shareholders normally do not have voting rights. *Preferred stock* has some of the features of a bond in that it pays a fixed dividend rate. It does not, however, have a maturity date.

Stock Dividend

Dividends received in the form of additional stock instead of cash are stock dividends. By declaring stock dividends, a company is increasing its total number of outstanding common stock. If the stock dividend is large enough, it is sometimes tantamount to a stock split. (See *Stock Split*.)

Stock Power

If you are selling stock you have in your own possession, you must deliver it to your broker by settlement date. Instead of sending it through the mail with your signature on it, your broker may ask you to sign a stock-power form and send the unsigned stock and the signed stock power to him in separate envelopes. This way, the stock is not negotiable until he receives both and clips them together.

Stock Rights

See *Rights*.

Stock Split

A stock split is different from a stock dividend in that it does not create an increase in the company's assets. If a company has one million shares of common outstanding, and it declares a two for one split, it will then have 2 million shares outstanding at half the par value of the original shares. The primary reason for doing this is to lower the price of the company's stock and make it more attractive to investors. In the case of a stock dividend, the par value is left unchanged and there is a resulting increase in the company's assets.

A *reverse spit* is just the opposite. There is a decrease in the number of shares with a proportionate increase in the par value of the stock. The effect here is to raise the price of the shares (See also *Par.*)

Stop Order

Suppose you bought a stock at 40 and watched it go to 55. You don't want to sell it yet, but neither do you want to lose your entire paper gain. You tell your broker to enter a stop order to sell at 50, which, if the stock should go down to 50, will trigger your order and your stock will be sold at the market. Conversely, you may have sold short at 55 and watched the stock fall to 40. You don't want to cover your short sale yet. So you tell your broker to enter a stop order to buy at 45, which will trigger a purchase if the stock should rise to that level.

A *stop-limit* order is similar, with one major exception. In the first instance above, if your order to sell had been a stop-limit, 50 will trigger a sale but you are telling the floor broker not to take less than 50 for the stock. This is riskier since, if the stock falls to 50, there is no guarantee that you can get 50 if there are other sell orders ahead of yours. The stock could keep falling all the way back to 40, and you will still be holding your stock. A stop order, on the other hand, guarantees an execution since it becomes a market order once the stock reaches 50.

Street Name

Instead of having securities registered in your own name and shipped to you, you might leave the securities with your broker in street name, registered in the brokerage firm's name for your account. This is especially useful if you are buying and selling on a regular basis, since it eliminates the trouble of shipping securities back and forth. You will receive statements periodically indicating that you are the owner of record.

Strike Price

A term used in options trading. When you buy a call or a put, you have the right to buy or sell a stock at a certain price by a specific date. Your target price—the one you can buy for or sell at—is the strike price. (See also *Call, Put, Option.*)

Support Level

Stand resistance level on its head and you have support level. It is the price at which, following a decline in the price of a stock, there is heavy buying into it that prevents any further decline. Literally, there is support for the stock at a particular price. It may drop from 30 to 22, at which point renewed buying begins to drive the price back up again. Again it falls and again it finds support at 22. If it should fall through 22 with any conviction, many chartists will regard it as an ominous sign that the stock will keep on dropping to a new low or until it finds a new or a previous support level. (See also *Chartist* and *Resistance Level.*)

Tape

Wall Street jargon for the string of numbers in your broker's office that reports transactions from the floors of the securities exchanges. At one time it was literally a tape; today it is electronic.

Tax-deferred

Income from securities on which you do not pay current taxes. The taxes are postponed or deferred to a later date.

Tax-free

Income from securities that is exempt from federal and, sometimes, from state and local income taxes.

Tax Shelter

An investment that permits you to get a tax write-off from pre-tax dollars. You are literally sheltering part of your income before the IRS can get hold of it. Tax-deferred and tax-free investments are usually made with after-tax dollars.

Technical Analysis

Technical analysts are concerned about the history of a stock's price movements and are not interested in the financial and economic fundamentals surrounding the issuing company. Their view is that price swings predate, or discount, the news. (See also *Chartist, Discount,* and *Fundamental Analysis.*)

Topping Out

A term used to describe a stock that has been rising in price but seems to be leveling off and establishing a plateau. The expectation is that the stock may soon begin to fall again. (See also *Bottoming Out.*)

Trading

A trading account is a speculative account. A trader is some-one who ordinarily buys and sells on a short-term basis in an attempt to realize quick profits.

Transaction

An order to buy or sell securities that is executed. The date of the transaction may be referred to as the trade date, execution date, or transaction date.

Treasuries

See *Bills*, *Bonds*, and *Notes*.

Trust

A trust is a set of written instructions directing that one's money or property be handled in a certain way. A trust can be either a *testamentary trust*, which is part of one's last will and testament, or a *living trust*, which goes into effect during the lifetime of the donor. (See also *Estate* and *Living Trust*.)

Underlying Stock

A call option involves the right to buy 100 shares of a specific stock at a specific price by a certain date. A put option involves the right to sell 100 shares of a specific stock at a specific price by a certain date. The specific stock in question in each option contract is known as the underlying stock. (See also *Call*, *Put*, and *Option*.)

Underwriter

In the securities business, the same thing as an investment banker. The investment bankers who form a syndicate to help an institution raise money are helping to underwrite the stocks or bonds being offered to the public.

Unsecured Bond

Also known as a debenture, backed only by the reputation and financial record of the company that issues it. It is not backed with physical assets, as is the case with secured bonds. (See also *Secured Bond*.)

Unit Investment Trust

Sometimes confused with a mutual fund, from which it differs in that it ordinarily issues shares of beneficial interest in a *fixed* portfolio of securities, and once these shares are sold, no additional shares are issued.

Uptick

An uptick is the opposite of a downtick; it is a rise in the price of a stock from its previous price. If a stock should rise from 34½ to 34¾, for example, it is upticking. (See also *Downtick*.)

Volume

Volume is the number of shares traded in the market or in a particular stock at any time during a trading day. Your broker can give you volume figures for different stocks and for the market in general by consulting his quote machine. If the market or a stock is going up on high volume, it is technically strong, a better sign than an advance on low volume. Likewise, a decline on high volume is considered a less happy sign than a decline on low or moderate volume. When you hear a market commentator say, "The market was up today but the advance was technically weak," he is referring to an advance on low volume.

Voting Trust Certificate (VTC)

Once in a while, when a company falls upon bad financial times, the shareholders may be asked to temporarily surrender their voting rights until the company puts itself in order again. When this happens, a bank may be appointed as trustee, and the stockholders could be asked to exchange their stock certificates for voting trust certificates. The stock remains on deposit with the bank until the trust is dissolved. The VTC is a receipt for the stock and carries all the rights of common stock except the right to vote, which has been surrendered to the trust. VTC's can be given away or sold just like common stock.

Warrant

A warrant is the right to buy a particular common stock at a price that is usually above the current market price. The warrant can expire at some future date, perhaps five or ten years off, or it may run in perpetuity. In a sense, a warrant is like a long-term call option. Warrants can be listed or traded over the counter like common stock. Their prices fluctuate from day to day with the price movements of the underlying securities. (See also *Call*.)

Wash Sale

A wash sale is a transaction that involves no change of beneficial ownership; there is no profit or loss involved. An order to buy and a simultaneous order to sell 100 shares of RCA at 27 which, in effect, cancel each other out, is considered a wash sale transaction. A series of wash sales in a particular security amounts to *painting the tape* (which see). Wash sales are sometimes made for tax purposes, and for this reason, the IRS will disallow certain transactions if they have some or all of the characteristics of a wash sale. For instance, if you sell stock to take a loss, the IRS will not allow the loss if you buy the same (or substantially the same) securities within thirty days before or after you sell for the loss.

When Issued

Securities can be traded among investors even though the actual certificates have not been printed yet. Stock received as a result of dividends or stock splits is a case in point. You will get the certificates when they are issued.

Wire Houses

Large brokerage firms with branch offices scattered throughout the country and in foreign countries are referred to as wire houses. The reason for this is that orders are wired in to the main office instead of entered via the telephone.

Writing Calls

If you own round lots of a stock and sell options on the stock, that is, sell the right for someone to buy the stock away from you at a set price by a particular date, you are writing calls. In options trading *writing* is synonomous with *selling*. (See also *Call*, *Put*, and *Option*.)

Writing Naked

Writing naked means you are selling calls on stock you do not own. This is a highly speculative maneuver in which the writer is gambling that the underlying stock will not go up before the expiration date, and he will not have to buy the stock in the market and sell it at a lower strike price. Writing naked can be done only in a margin account. (See also *Call*.).

Yield

Yield is the return you are getting from your investment. A stock may be said to be yielding 3, 5, or 9 percent, which is figured by dividing the price of the stock into the dividend payment per share.

In the case of *bond yield*, there are three basic measurements. *Nominal yield* is the original coupon yield or the yield when the bond is at par—9 percent, or $90, a year per $1000 for example.

Current yield is the actual yield you are getting based on the present market price. If the above bond were trading at $900, the current yield to you would be 10 percent, or $90, a year for a $900 investment.

Yield-to-maturity takes into consideration the current yield and the capital gain or loss you will have when the bond matures. Look again at *current yield*, above. In addition to getting a 10 percent a year current return, you will also have a $100 capital gain upon redemption. This gain is figured into your current yield to give you your yield-to-maturity.

Now Let's Begin

You and I have taken a rather long journey together in a fairly brief period of time and space. We started from ground zero and covered the basics of the securities investment world step by step. My intention was to convey information and knowledge that I have acquired over a few years in the business in a straightforward, easy-to-understand manner. Only you can say whether or not I have succeeded.

Although we are now at the end of our journey, I would like to think that we have really come to something of a new beginning. The investment world—and the broader topic of money, itself—is something we should all remain familiar with as we grow and prosper through life. We work hard for the money we bring in, and it is important to understand the best ways of putting it to work for us. The whole purpose of working to earn a living is defeated if we permit ourselves to lose ground to inflation each year, if we do not get the best possible return we can from the dollars we earn.

The investment world has something to offer all of us, cautious conservative, moderate risk-taker looking for growth, and action-oriented speculator alike. This is perhaps the main reason why it is such a fascinating world. It is full of details and can appear complicated at times, yet there is a logic to it that makes these details easy to grasp with a bit of application. All of us can master it, and really must master it if we expect to handle our money in a sensible fashion. We all owe it to ourselves to become financially literate, and I hope this book makes that task a little easier.

When you feel that you are ready for more advanced reading in this area, there are dozens of sophisticated books that cover different aspects of the investment world. This book has, I hope, taught you how to walk, how to get started. Regard it as a launching pad. From here, when you are ready, you can spring off in any direction that suits you.

In this regard, I do not feel my job is finished with the completion of this book. If you have any questions that need answering, any problems you need assistance with, I would like to put my own abilities at your disposal. You can start by directing your queries to me in care of Collier Associates, 280 Madison Avenue, New York, NY 10016. If I cannot reply to you myself, I will see to it that any questions or problems you have are passed along to someone who can help you.

So let's end it here for the moment. Let's end it at the beginning. A new universe is now waiting to be explored. Here's to an exciting and rewarding journey into the future.

Index